IMAGINE WHAT CHANGE COULD MEAN!

- *Imagine* making plans, confident that you have the best possible chance of carrying them through
- *Imagine* not being forced to face the anxiety of missed deadlines, and crisis after crisis
- *Imagine* not having to make excuses for not finishing a job
- *Imagine* having the time, energy, and enthusiasm to enjoy what you're doing

IMAGINE HOW GOOD IT FEELS TO— *GET IT DONE!*

D1616996

GET IT DONE!

A GUIDE TO MOTIVATION, DETERMINATION AND ACHIEVEMENT

IAN McMAHAN, Ph.D.

AVON BOOKS ◆ NEW YORK

VISIT OUR WEBSITE AT
http://AvonBooks.com

GET IT DONE! is an original publication of Avon Books. This work has never before appeared in book form.

AVON BOOKS
A division of
The Hearst Corporation
1350 Avenue of the Americas
New York, New York 10019

Copyright © 1996 by Ian McMahan
Published by arrangement with the author
Library of Congress Catalog Card Number: 96-96451
ISBN: 0-380-77970-6

First Avon Books Printing: November 1996

AVON TRADEMARK REG. U.S. PAT. OFF. AND IN OTHER COUNTRIES, MARCA REGISTRADA, HECHO EN U.S.A.

Printed in the U.S.A.

RA   10 9 8 7 6 5 4 3 2 1

This book is dedicated to my wife, Jane, and my daughter, Selena. I could always rely on both of them, whenever my energy or enthusiasm flagged, to tell me, "Come on, just *get it done!*"

CONTENTS

1

GETTING IT DONE: WHAT'S IN YOUR WAY?

What do you want?

You already know some answers to that question. You want to be more effective, more secure, more alive. You want to get things done, and not just anything, but the things you *want* to get done. You want to feel better about your successes and not brood so much about your failures. You want to approach new challenges more in the spirit of a kid who has just been given a new puzzle, and less in the spirit of someone who has just spotted an envelope in the mail with an IRS return address.

You are also someone who believes—or who'd very much like to believe—that *we can change*, that we don't have to live with old patterns and habits that get in our way. If you weren't, I doubt you would have even noticed this book. You certainly wouldn't have picked it up and read this far. By doing so, you've taken a first step toward becoming someone who knows how to *Get It Done*.

Now take a second step. Read the next section, or the next few sections, of this chapter. They'll give you a clearer idea of what this book is about and what it can do for you. But please, don't sit down and read through the whole book at one time, or even over a few days. The process is a little like watering a flower bed. If you don't give the water time to sink in, most of it will run off and leave the flowers as thirsty as ever.

Dropping Out

David was a student in my Adolescent Psychology course. When he came by during my office hours, I thought he was there to check out a topic for his term paper. Instead, he perched awkwardly on the edge of his chair, stared at the floor, and said, "I think I'm going to drop out of college."

"Oh?" I replied. I tried to keep the surprise and dismay out of my voice. I knew David was a serious student, hardworking and earnest, if a little dogged. I also knew, from some of our discussions in class, that his getting a college degree meant a lot to him and his family.

"I just can't hack it," he continued. "I'm carrying two Incompletes from last term. If I don't get the term papers in by next month, the I's turn into F's, and there goes my grade point average. I'd rather drop out than flunk out."

I asked, "What about those papers? Can't you do them in time? Or get an extension on them?"

David shook his head. "I've done most of the research," he said. "But, I don't know . . . every time I try to sit down and look over my notes, I panic. I'll never be able to do them. And even if I did, what's the point? They won't be any good.''

"How were you doing before the two Incompletes?" I asked.

"Okay, I guess," he replied with a shrug. "Mostly B's, a few A's, and a couple of C's."

"That's a lot better than just okay," I pointed out. "With those grades, you could graduate with honors."

"I guess," he repeated, with another shrug. "But I can't keep it up. Every time I get a good grade, my heart sinks. I figure it's just a matter of time before it catches up with me."

He paused, then added, "It's funny—I always knew I wanted to go to college. But now . . . I don't know what I expected, but it's turned into just one long grind. I'm not getting anything out of it. And where's it leading? What's the point?"

Before David left my office, I gave him some advice about how to set priorities. I also lent him a book about efficient study habits. I hope the advice and the book helped. I do know that he completed the semester and got a B in my course.

Later, though, as I thought about what had been said, I began to wonder if my advice, and that book I'd lent him, hadn't been beside the point. There was nothing wrong with the advice or the book, but they had been aimed at the wrong target. David's problem wasn't a lack of organization or good study skills. It was the way he thought and felt about school, and grades, and his successes and failures. In other words, it was a question of his *motivation*.

David . . . and You

Your college days may be long behind you, but that doesn't mean you've left behind the sorts of difficulties that David was having. Ask yourself a few questions.

- Do you have trouble getting started on a project, whether it's work-related, social, or personal?

- Once you do get started, do you find yourself thrown by even minor setbacks and obstacles?

- Are you convinced that you need the pressure of a deadline to get anything done?

- When you do finish a project, do you feel drained?

- Has an opportunity ever slipped by because you couldn't organize yourself to take advantage of it?

- Do you have important plans and activities— important *to you*—that keep getting put off to some time in the future?

If you answered "yes" to some, or most, of these questions, don't worry—you're not alone. Many of us have problems of this sort. And let's be very clear about one thing from the start. They *are* problems. They're not simply a result of "the way things are." It's much more accurate to say that they're a result of the way *we* are.

Over a lifetime, we've built up a web of motivational habits. These habits determine what we expect when we approach something new, the kinds of chal-

lenges we're attracted to, the reasons we give ourselves for our successes and failures, even the reasons
we give ourselves for doing anything at all. When we
try to do something, these habits can trip us up and
send us sprawling. They are so deeply rooted, so en-
twined with our basic idea of who we are, that we
probably don't even notice them unless someone
points them out. And even then, we can't help be-
lieving that everyone else has them, too.

Okay, we know a few people who seem different.
Somehow they always manage to get things done.
There's my friend, Frank, for example. He has a busy
law practice, coaches his daughter's soccer team, does
volunteer work with a community organization, has a
wide circle of friends, and still manages to keep up
with the books, films, and plays that I never find the
time for. Even more infuriating, he seems to enjoy
every minute of it. How does he do it? Is it all a front?
Was he just born lucky?

Whatever the answer, we know that *we* certainly
aren't like that. What's more, we can't imagine that
we ever could be.

Wrong. We can be that way. It isn't easy, of course.
Think how long we've spent becoming the way we
are now. But with the right approach, with an understanding of what works for us and what works against
us, and with a lot of determination and hard work, *we
can choose to change*. We can conquer our old, un-
productive, unrewarding patterns and create new ones.

Imagine what that could mean:

- Not being forced to trudge through our daily
  lives feeling ground down by deadline after
  deadline, crisis after crisis, unfinished task after unfinished task.

- Being able to make plans, both short-term and long-term, with the knowledge that we are giving ourselves the best possible chance of carrying them through.

- Having the time, energy, and positive attitudes that allow us, not only to do more of what we want and enjoy, but to want and enjoy more of what we do.

"I'm as Motivated as Anyone, But . . ."

Ask anyone you know if he or she is motivated. Chances are, the answer you get will be yes. And not just plain yes, but "Yes, of course!" with a look that says that you're a little odd even to ask the question. Yet a lot of the time, we know things about our friend that tell us it just isn't so. Why is it so hard for people to admit that they have problems with motivation?

The answer isn't hard to find. Most of us have grown up thinking that there is something disgraceful about being unmotivated. Don't we all understand that calling someone "unmotivated" is simply a nicer, more polite way of saying "lazy?" And people who are lazy get no sympathy.

All of us go around with our own personal theories of human psychology. You don't have to take a course in psychology to have one. You've been working on yours ever since you were a little kid. When a playmate bumped into you and knocked you down, you used your theory to get answers to some very urgent questions. Did she mean to hurt you? Should you push her back? Was she still your friend?

Even as adults, these personal psychological theories play a big role in our decisions about others: why they act the way they do, what they are likely to do next, how we should act toward them to get the results we want. Call it "street smarts," or "intuition," or "a shrewd grasp of character," it's really the same function.

One interesting fact is that most people in our culture end up with pretty much the *same* personal theory of psychology. And according to that theory, "motivation" is something that is basically under our own personal control. People assume that you can *decide* to be motivated or not. That means that you are responsible for your motivation or lack of it. If you're not motivated, you don't have a problem, you have a weak character.

Suppose you promised to give a friend a lift to work, and you don't show up. If the reason is that your car wouldn't start, your friend will probably excuse you (though he might grouse that you should keep your car in better shape). But if you couldn't bring yourself to get out of bed, how do you think he'll react to *that* excuse? In his place, how would you react?

Since people generally think this way, the result is that it feels risky to admit that you might have a motivational problem. "Oh?" we can hear them saying. "Well, in that case, why don't you just fix it? What's the matter? Don't you have any willpower? Pull yourself up by your bootstraps."

(By the way, if you stop to think about it, you'll notice that the expression, "Pull yourself up by your bootstraps," means to do something that everyone knows is, not just difficult, but literally *impossible*.)

A motivational problem feels so much like a per-

sonal failing that we even try to hide it from ourselves. We decide that, whatever the difficulty is, we
can overcome it by simply putting our mind to it.
Where there's a will, there's a way. So we give it our
best shot—and it doesn't work. At that point, we start
groping for other explanations, and sooner or later,
we find them. They may be almost as well-worn as
"The dog ate my term paper," and not much more
convincing, but that's all right. The important thing is
that they feel less shameful and easier to live with
than the other possibility—that we are simply weak-
willed.

"I Don't Have Enough Time"

My week has 168 hours in it, no more, no less. So
does yours. And we need at least a few of those hours
for sleeping, eating, brushing our teeth, walking the
dog, etc. It sounds perfectly reasonable to say that our
difficulties in getting things done come from a lack
of time. If only we had more time, or if we used our
time better, we *would* get them done.

Then along comes a three-day weekend, or a snow-
storm shuts down the office, or you go on vacation.
Suddenly, you do have more time. What happens? Do
you become a whirlwind of energy, whizzing through
all those projects that you've been putting off because
you didn't have the time to get to them? Or do you
find that it's still just as hard as ever?

Changing your motivational patterns will not put
more hours in your week. What it can do, however,
is help you use, and experience, your hours differently.

When you are totally engaged in something that you want to do, unfettered by conflicting fears and expectations, time takes on a different meaning. You come to a pause, look up, and realize that hours have gone by without your noticing.

On the other hand, we all know what it's like to be doing something only because we have to. Like a road across Kansas, each minute seems to stretch on forever, from here to the horizon. Forget about having too little time. When we are not motivated from within, there is more time than anyone could want— and no one wants it.

"I Don't Have Enough Energy"

The other day, I asked my daughter to set the table for dinner. "Oh, Daddy, I can't," she said in a piteous voice. "I'm, like, totally exhausted."

Since she was still getting over a bout of flu, I shrugged, said, "Okay," and set the table myself.

A few minutes later, a friend called and asked her over to play. What a marvelous, almost instantaneous recovery!

I want to be very careful here, because there's a good chance that, sooner or later, my daughter will read these words. I am *not* saying that she was faking when she told me she was exhausted. I'm quite sure that she really did feel that way. I too often feel tired when I think about doing chores. I usually do them anyway, because I've gradually learned that getting them out of the way is less tiring than putting them off, then brooding about not doing them. But I didn't know that at her age, or even at twice her age.

And the recovery was certainly genuine. When she had a chance to do something she really wanted to do, she found the energy to do it, as we all have in similar situations. Now look at it from the other direction. What if there's something you consistently put off doing because you *don't* have the energy? Assuming that you're in reasonable health, getting a reasonable amount of sleep, and eating a fairly healthy diet, the conclusion seems obvious. You don't really want to do whatever it is. If you did, you'd find the energy.

The problem with this argument is that it leaves out the element of *conflict*. Motivation is not simply a matter of wants. It is also about fears, doubts, and the collisions among different wants, fears, and doubts. Just wanting something isn't enough to give you the energy to do it. The energy you need may be blocked by other things within your motivational structure.

On the other hand, if we do find the energy to do some things and not others, the problem obviously isn't lack of energy in general. Instead, it has to do with the way energy is being doled out. And that, as we'll see, is very much a question of motivation.

"It's Not Rewarding Enough"

In one of R. Crumb's comic strips, his character, Mr. Natural, confronts a sink piled high with dirty dishes. Grumbling, he rolls up his sleeves and gets to work. The longer it takes, the more he grumbles. At last the sink is empty. The drying rack is neatly stacked with clean dishes. Mr. Natural smiles as he walks away, saying, "A job well done."

That's a nice way to feel when you finish something. But notice that Crumb doesn't show Mr. Natural as being thrilled while he's actually washing the dishes. And too often, both the doing *and* the finishing come to seem, in Hamlet's words, "weary, stale, flat, and unprofitable."

Why is what you're doing so unrewarding? It may be something about the activity itself. Some tasks are more exciting, more engaging than others. In filmmaking, not everyone can be a director or actor. Somebody has to load the cameras, and someone has to keep track of the number of sandwiches the cast and crew eat at lunch. Even the star spends hours on end waiting around for some minor problem to be taken care of.

What you're doing doesn't explain it all, though. Just out of high school, I spent a summer working in a service station in West Texas. It was not a glamorous job. Customers would pull in after an hour or two of highway driving. In return for buying three bucks worth of Ethyl, they expected you to check the oil, the radiator, and the pressure in their tires—and scrape a quarter-inch-thick layer of dead bugs off the windshield.

After eight hours of this, I was usually a zombie—a hyperactive zombie, thanks to all the Cokes I'd drunk to keep going. Not Steve, the assistant manager. He ended his shift as fresh as when he'd started it, and not by delegating the dirty jobs, either. He actually seemed to *like* polishing windshields. A lot of the time he'd go on to clean the customer's headlights as well.

Once, when we were both on the midnight-to-eight shift and business was slow, I asked him what his secret was. He scratched his cheek and said, "No secret to it, Skip. This is a service station. The way I see it, we ought to be glad when folks give us a chance to do them a service.''

In other words, he got satisfaction from his work, not because it was any less dirty and tiring than the work the rest of us were doing, but because he looked at it in a different way. That has an important, even radical implication. It's not the job itself that is rewarding or unrewarding, so much as the way we think and feel about it. And *that* is a product of our motivational patterns and styles.

"Motivational Techniques Don't Work For Me"

There's one thing I should make clear right off. This is *not* a book about time management. If you're like me, you already have a few of those on your bookshelves. Every year or so, you pick up a new one. Maybe a friend recommends it. Or maybe you notice an ad or review that makes it sound exactly like what you need. You read it eagerly, and for the next few days you feel inspired. Your self-confidence soars.

This time, you know it's going to work. You will get your files reorganized, your to-do lists in order, your short- and long-term priorities straight. You even go out and buy an *n*th-generation appointment book or a personal information management program for your computer that promises to make organizing your life easy, effective, and fun.

You know what happens next. After a week or so, the lift you got from reading the new book has somehow seeped away. Like that balloon your kid brought home from a birthday party, your spirits gradually sink from the ceiling to somewhere near the floor.

Those files you started to reorder and consolidate? They're sitting in a pile on the corner of your desk, gathering dust. That new appointment book will be an enormous help—if you can ever find the time to finish transferring the information you need from your old one.

And when you read back over your to-do lists, you notice that you've checked off all the simple items: *straighten desk*, *mail bills*, *pick up cleaning*. Terrific. But the items that really count, the ones that call for close attention or a long-term effort, keep getting moved from yesterday's list to today's, and then to tomorrow's. And each time they are moved to another day's (or week's, or month's!) to-do list, you feel that much less confidence that you will *ever* be able to get them done.

I am not saying, of course, that the effort you put into learning about time management techniques is wasted. Let's put it this way. If you decide to build a backyard fence or a doghouse, you don't start by reinventing hammers, saws, and nails. You hunt up a how-to book—or a live expert—and find out what tools you'll need and how to use them properly.

It's the same with, say, finding places to put all those maddening but important pieces of paper. You could do what a lot of us do—shove them in a box, then stick the box in a closet. At least they're out of sight. But this doesn't help you when you have to fill out your tax return or you want to take another look at your son's report card from last year. You could invent your own filing system, based on your astrological chart or the letters in your mother's maiden name. But you needn't bother. Intelligent people have spent whole careers developing better ways to organize, store, and retrieve documents. It makes the best of sense to take advantage of their work. But to do that, *we have to do it*.

I used to know a lawyer who felt that he needed a hobby to take his mind off the stresses of his high-powered career. For some reason, he decided to take up marquetry. That's the art of inlaying carefully-shaped pieces of different-colored woods to form intricate designs or pictures.

He called the three main American sources of wood-inlay supplies and asked for their catalogues. After studying them, he ordered a Swedish workbench, an assortment of thin sheets of exotic woods, a set of English veneering knives, some very specialized clamps, and various glues, rollers, and books of designs.

I'm sure you've already guessed the end of the story. The last I heard, all that expensive equipment was sitting in a corner of his basement, gathering dust.

It may be an obvious point, but it's worth emphasizing: *No matter how many high-tech tools we buy, no matter how many advanced organizational techniques we learn, they won't do us any good unless we also have the motivation to* use *them*.

"I Can't Help The Way I Am"

- Sure I'm easily distracted. It runs in my family. My mother was exactly the same way.

- How can you expect me to have any real self esteem, after the way I was treated as a child?

- The reason I can't get ahead is that my boss has it in for me.
- I know my kid's doing badly in school, but it's not his fault or mine. Look at the way the schools have gone downhill in the past few years.

You have probably heard people say things like that often. You have probably heard *yourself* say them just as often. I know I catch myself doing it at least several times a day, and those are just the times when I *do* catch myself.

What all these statements have in common is that they reflect a particular way of looking at the world. This point of view, which philosophers call *determinism*, says that everything we do and think and feel is a direct reaction to what happens to us and the way we are. We may have the illusion that we are making choices, but even our choices are really determined. So is our belief that we are choosing.

Here are the real messages in these statements:

- I am the way I am because of the genes I inherited from my parents and more distant ancestors.
- I am the way I am because things that happened in my past made my personality take a certain shape.
- I am the way I am because forces in my environment—the culture, the economy, the people around me—make me that way.
- I am the way I am because of the combination of my genes, my past, and the environment around me.

And all these messages also carry two important implications that usually remain unspoken:

- I can't be held responsible for the way I am.
- I can't do anything to change the way I am.

It should be obvious that if I really believed these messages, I'd have no business writing a book aimed at helping people to change. And if you really believe them, and you're not ready to consider the possibility that they're mistaken, what on earth are you doing *reading* such a book?

I am not about to get into a discussion of "free will," but I would like to make one important point. Research has shown that people who believe they have no choice act differently from those who believe they have the ability to decide what to do. And the differences almost always give an advantage to those who believe they can decide. So whether we "really" have that ability or not, we're better off if we take it as given and *use it*.

The Ability to Choose

Man is neither as free as he feels nor as bound as he fears.

—*Silvan Tomkins*

A deterministic philosophy leaves out a few very important factors. As humans, we have the amazing ability to become aware of ourselves, to think about who we are and what we are doing, and to imagine how we might be different. If I usually resent it when my supervisor makes a suggestion, I can notice that and imagine myself being more cooperative. And I can *choose* to make an effort to change.

This does not mean we can freely choose to be who and what we want. Anyone who's ever made a New Year's resolution to give up cigarettes knows better than that. We can choose, yes, but making our choice *stick* is not so easy. In the case of smoking, we're fighting a set of habits that goes back years, and a physical dependency as well.

Our genetic background, our childhood, our environment—all these have real power over us. Don't underestimate that power. Challenging it is hard, sometimes impossible work. You may love horses and long to be a professional jockey. But if your genes have made you a six-foot-one, two-hundred-pounder, I'm sorry, but you are out of luck. Racehorses don't come in your size.

What if you're a poor, undereducated teenager in a black ghetto? You were malnourished as a child, and perhaps abused as well. Your neighborhood is full of drugs, guns, and rats. Among your older friends, more are going to prison than to college. Can you still choose to stay clear of trouble with the law, and even to train yourself for a profession?

Yes, you can. I've had some outstanding students in my classes who are doing just that. I admire their determination and honor the struggle they've had and are still having. But it also makes me sad. How much easier it would have been for them if they had grown up in a stable, peaceful neighborhood and gone to schools where they were expected to succeed. And how many others there are who also might have chosen and achieved a better life if the forces against it hadn't been too strong for them.

What You Can Expect From This Book

The goal of this book is to show you, through real life examples and practical exercises, how to put the insights of motivational psychology to work for you. First, we'll get acquainted with the basic principles of motivation and motivational change. Next, we'll take a detailed look at the five critical factors that influence our motivation to get things done. Finally, we'll see how the effort we put into developing our motivation to achieve also sets us on the path toward the larger goals of personal growth and self-determination.

Here are quick previews of the individual chapters.

The next chapter poses the question, "How Can We Change?" and presents some answers to it. Are we forever trapped by the traits that we inherited from our parents or developed in early childhood? If we decide that we want and need to change, what are the tools we must have? What goals will we set for ourselves, and how? How will we know if we are going in the right direction, and how will we know when we get there?

In Chapter Three, we meet the first of the five critical factors, *expectations*. We see how expectations have a major impact on what we do and what happens to us. We learn about the "Pygmalion effect" and self-fulfilling prophecies. Finally, we find out how to evaluate our patterns of expectations, then to change them.

The second critical factor, *achievement motivation*,

is the focus of Chapter Four. What does it indicate when someone chooses very easy or almost impossible tasks? When is persistence a virtue, and when is it a means of escape? How can we start to alter our basic achievement motives, and what benefits can we expect when we do?

Chapter Five looks at the explanations we give ourselves for our successes and failures. Why do these *attributions* affect the way we feel about our outcomes and how hard we'll try next time—if we try at all? What are the different attributional styles, and what are their effects? Are you an ''internal'' or an ''external?'' How can we change the way we think about the results of what we do?

In Chapter Six, we look at the different ways people structure long range tasks and what the effects of these ways are. Is there anything we can do to keep our motivation high when we're working toward a goal that may take weeks, months, or even years to reach? What are *interim goals and rewards*, and why are they so important?

Is it possible to turn work into play? Is it desirable? How do we go about doing it? Those are among the questions we'll talk about in Chapter Seven. We'll discuss different kinds of rewards, and why they have such different effects on our motivation. And we'll learn new ways of thinking about what we do, ways that make us more productive and make what we do more fun.

In the last chapter, we'll try to put everything we've learned into a larger context. How do you see yourself: as a pawn in someone else's game or as a player with the power to determine what happens? Where does your sense of self-worth come from, and what is it based on? Is it true that "to the victor belong the spoils," or are some things more important than winning? And once you've seen for yourself that it is *possible* to change, where do you go from here?

2

SEVEN STEPS TO PERSONAL CHANGE

For every path into the forest, a path out of the forest.

—*Old Irish saying*

We know that we're not really happy with the way we are. We know that we want to change. But it isn't so obvious how to get from here to there, especially if we're not quite sure where either *here* or *there* is.

When I was twelve, my Boy Scout troop took part in an orienteering contest. Each group of five or six kids was given maps, compasses, and a course to follow, and dropped off along the edge of a big patch of dense woods. The object was to come out on the other side of the woods at the spot marked on our map.

If you've never tried it, that may sound pretty easy. Believe me, it isn't. Even following a compass bearing across an open field can get tricky. And when you're in a shadowy, overgrown forest and the course you've set vanishes into an impenetrable thicket, and

21

your attempt to go around the thicket leads you straight into a swamp. . . .

After nearly an hour of wandering around, slapping at hungry mosquitoes and using the kind of language that Boy Scouts weren't supposed to know, my group found itself standing at the edge of a winding stream. We were obviously lost. The contest was obviously lost, too. Not that we cared very much at that point. We were too busy wondering whether we would find our way back to camp in time for supper—or at all!

Then my friend, Sandy, took a closer look at the map. The stream was clearly marked on it. Of the bends shown, only one had the shape of the one we were standing next to. When Sandy pointed this out, the rest of us looked, too. He was right.

So we weren't lost after all. It's true we didn't know how we had gotten there, but we did know *where we were*. We also knew *where we wanted to go*. And those two facts were all we really needed to find our way out of the woods. Another half hour of sweaty trudging brought us out onto the road, not that far from the place we had been aiming for in the first place.

I believe your situation is like the one my orienteering team found itself in. To change effectively, you need to find out *where you are* and *where you want to go*. You also need to find out how you *got* to where you are. The answer to that problem isn't as easily determined.

Over a hundred years ago, Sigmund Freud, the founder of psychoanalysis, told the world that the first step in changing a person's psychological patterns was to trace those patterns back to their starting points. If you're terrified of flying, for example, you might try to recall when you first felt that fear, what other fears flying is connected to in your mind, and so on. Once you uncover the roots of the problem, you can begin to deal with it as an adult and not as the child you were at the time you developed the problem.

As Freud continued his investigations of the mind, he came to believe that the process was much more complicated and difficult than simply tracing the history of a pattern or problem. Even so, the idea of gaining *insight* into the sources of one's thoughts, feelings, and ways of behaving remained a basic goal. It is still an important element in many different approaches to therapy, recovery, and self-help.

Nonetheless, this idea still leaves us to face a couple of crucial questions.

- If there's something about ourselves that we want to change, do we *have* to find out where it came from before we can change it?

- If we *do* manage to discover where it came from, will that actually help us change it?

A good deal of psychological research suggests that the best answer to both these questions is, "No." We *can* overcome a problem or habit without knowing where we got it from. However, simply finding out where we got it from won't necessarily help us to change it. For example:

Joan runs the corporate desk at a large, multi-office travel agency. Her superiors think highly of her, and if you press her, even she will admit that she's good at her job. But more than once, when she's had a chance to move up the ladder, she has backed away.

A couple of years in therapy have helped Joan see that while she was growing up, her father constantly belittled her achievements and her abilities. He himself never went as far in his career as everybody had predicted he would, and he apparently deflected his disappointment and bitterness over this onto his daughter.

"I feel better, now that I'm beginning to understand why I'm the way I am," Joan recently told her best friend, Michele. "But frankly, not as much better as I'd like. I mean, let's say I'm on my way home today and I get hit by a truck. I'm knocked unconscious and both my legs are broken. I come to in the hospital. I discover I can't walk, and I haven't the least idea how I got that way. Am I going to want to know what happened to me? You better believe I am! I'm going to want the name of a good personal-injuries lawyer, too. But do you know what'll be the absolute number one on my list of things to find out? How to get better. What do I have to do to walk again?"

Three Urgent Questions

Joan's experience with therapy, like my early adventure in pathfinding, gives us some valuable insights into the process of change. Whether we decide to explore where our habits and problems came from or to set that aside for the time being, we still have at least three urgent questions.

1. Where are we now? What are the problems or difficulties that we want to do something about? What are the strengths we have to work *with*, and what are the weaknesses we have to work *on*?

2. Where do we want to get to? Unless we have pretty clear and concrete ideas about our goals, how will we know when we've reached them? How will we even know if we're going toward them, and not in a totally different direction?

3. What paths lead from here to there? And once we've found *that* out, how do we decide which one is the best path for us?

In some situations, coming up with answers to these questions isn't that hard. Imagine that you, like Joan in her analogy, woke up in a hospital bed with both your legs in casts. You'd know exactly where you were: in a hospital bed with a lot of stiff, plaster-soaked gauze wrapped around you. And you wouldn't find it hard to spell out where you wanted to get to, either: out, home, with both legs working just as well as they did before. As for finding out how to get from here to there, you would ask for advice from professionals—orthopedists, physical therapists—who know the way and who would make it their business to point it out and help you along.

Unfortunately, when we're talking about changing our motivational patterns, it's not so straightforward. All three of our questions turn out to call for thought and effort if we want to do a good job of answering them.

Where Am I Starting From?

It may seem strange, but we don't necessarily know what our motivational patterns really are. For example, most people will tell you that they are motivated to succeed; however, as we'll see in a later chapter, a closer look at the way people behave shows that many of them are actually acting under the influence of very different motives.

They were not fooling themselves or shading the truth about their motives, however. It's simply that we are not in the habit of looking closely at the long-term patterns in our actions and trying to understand what they mean. Instead, we simply take it for granted that we're pretty much like other people we know.

Even when we begin to look, uncovering our motivations isn't always easy. A broken leg will show up on an x-ray, but there is no magic device that will give us clear, sharp pictures of our motives and expectations. Even the best measures that psychologists have come up with offer results more like snapshots from a disposable camera: recognizable, but blurry.

There's another complication as well. It's called the principle of *overdetermination*. Whatever we do, whatever choices we make, we're usually acting on the basis of more than one motive at the same time. But as a rule, we pay attention to only one—the strongest, maybe, or the most obvious, or the one that makes us feel better about ourselves. The others stay half-hidden and unidentified.

Let's say I decide to go to a movie next Saturday. In no particular order, my motivations might include:

- I've heard good things about the film and I think I'll enjoy it.

- I know people at work will be talking about the film and I don't want to feel left out of the discussion.

- It's a good chance to do something fun with the person I'm planning to go with.

- It's a way to take my mind off some problems that have been bothering me.

- I'm trying to lose weight, but when I go to a movie I feel I have the right to indulge in a big bucket of popcorn *with* buttery topping.

The real reason may be any or all of these, or others that I haven't even thought of. That's the point. I have to realize that more than one motive may be at work, and to keep on looking after noticing the most obvious ones.

Identifying Motivational Patterns

How can we go about becoming aware of our motivational patterns? What tools can we use to make the job easier and quicker, so that we can move on toward our main goal of *changing* those patterns? Here are a couple of suggestions.

Take notes. It's a simple idea, but it works surprisingly well. Whenever you read or hear something that rings a bell, something that makes you think, "I've acted exactly that way myself," make a note of it.

As you read through this book, for example, keep a Hi-Lighter handy. Any time you come across a phrase or sentence that seems especially relevant or meaningful to you, mark it.

Better still, start a notebook. Get one that's small enough to carry around with you. Copy those significant passages into it. The physical act of writing them down will plant them more firmly in your mind than underlining ever could.

At the same time, try to summarize the passages or put them into your own words. This effort will make the ideas stick even better. It's also a good way of checking yourself and making sure you really understood what you read.

After you've done this for a little while, take a quiet moment to read through your notebook. If there is a pattern or common thread to the ideas you found relevant, that may be a good clue to your motivational makeup.

Let's say that you find you've copied twice as many passages that deal with failure than with success. That suggests that you're someone who is more concerned about the possible costs of failure than with the possible rewards of success.

Your notebook can be valuable in another way, too. As you work on changing your motivational patterns, the ideas that you find significant are likely to change, too. You'll be able to chart those changes and see where you've come from and where you've got to.

Assess yourself. Throughout this book, you'll find a variety of self-assessment tools. These have been freely adapted from measures that motivational and personality psychologists have developed over the years.

These are *not* tests of your knowledge or intelligence. You don't get a grade, there's no passing mark, and you won't be put on a scale with other people. We're a long way from the sort of "Test Your Organizational IQ'' feature you might come across in a supermarket magazine.

What are these tools good for? Imagine that someone leads you into a darkened theater. In front of you is the board that controls the stage lighting. You press a switch, and a bluish light comes on for a moment, aimed at the left side of the stage set. Another switch turns on a yellow light, pointed toward the upper part of the set. Still another is red and focused tightly on a single desk chair.

Each of the lights shows you only a little of the set and its furnishings. But gradually, you begin to get a sense of the set as a whole. The lights do not create the stage set. What they do is reveal different parts of it in new, different ways. They guide your attention to objects and angles and relationships that you might not have noticed without them.

The psychological measures in this book are similar. Their purpose is to highlight things about your thoughts, feelings, and actions that affect your motivation. These are things you may never have noticed before. Maybe you didn't happen to ask yourself the right questions. Maybe you did notice them, but didn't think that they were of any real significance. Once you see them and begin to understand what they mean, you gain new knowledge about your psychological functioning.

Where Do I Want to Go?

> *''Would you tell me, please, which way I ought to walk from here?''*
>
> *''That depends a good deal on where you want to get to,'' said the Cat.*

"I don't much care where—" said Alice.

"Then it doesn't matter which way you go," said the Cat.

"—so long as I get somewhere,*"* Alice added as an explanation.

"Oh, you're sure to do that," said the Cat, *"if you only walk long enough."*

—Lewis Carroll,
Alice's Adventures in Wonderland

Like Alice when she was lost in Wonderland, most of us would love to find someone to tell us which way we ought to go. It's not hard to find someone who's willing to try it, either. The trouble is, their advice generally turns out to be like the advice of the Cheshire Cat—sensible, maybe, but totally useless as a guide.

After all, the Cheshire Cat is right. The path we take really does depend on where we want to get to. And until we have a pretty clear idea of where that is, it is tough to know if we're going in the right direction.

In a way, people who are trying to stop smoking are lucky. They know exactly what their goal is—not to smoke—and they have an easy way to tell if they are getting closer to or farther from that goal. All they need to do is keep an honest count of how many cigarettes they smoke.

(Please understand, I'm not saying that the *process* of giving up smoking is easy. As an ex-smoker myself, I know how hard it can be. But even when I was going through two packs of unfiltered cigarettes a day, I knew that what I wanted to do was to quit. I may not have believed that I could ever reach that goal, but I certainly knew what it was.)

Instead of setting the goal of not smoking, let's say you decided that what you wanted was to breathe more easily, enjoy the taste of your meals and the scents of a spring garden, and be able to take a brisk walk without wheezing. Chances are, it won't work. You'll become discouraged well before you reach your goals because, although these are among the likely results of not smoking, you don't get them until well *after* you've stopped smoking. Even if you manage to quit for a week or two, your system won't have had time to detoxify. Thus, quitting didn't get you where you expected it to. And the next time you get tense, you'll probably reach for a cigarette.

People who are working on changing their motivational patterns can fall into a similar trap. It's easy to list some of the results we'd like to see. We want to:

- stop putting things off
- approach new tasks with a confident, upbeat attitude
- put more zest into what we do, and get more pleasure out of doing it
- choose tasks that help us both to succeed more often and to take more pride in our successes
- stop worrying so much about our failures
- avoid discouragement and a loss of self-confidence
- be more creative
- pay more attention and devote more effort to what really counts in our lives

and so on, and so on.

Every one of these goals is worthwhile. Most of them can be reached by people who succeed in changing the motivational habits that have been holding them back. But they don't come instantly. They are among the long-term consequences of a process. If we think of them as the goals we're setting out to achieve, we may find that they always seem just over the horizon, just beyond the next bend, and never at hand. At that point, the temptation to give up, to fall back into the same negative ways of thinking that we'd hoped to escape, will be very hard to resist.

Set concrete goals. An alternative approach to goal setting is modeled after the example of someone who wants to quit smoking. What it requires is choosing a goal that is concrete enough to be *observed* and *measured*.

When I'm writing, I sometimes get stuck hunting for the best way to express what I want to say. To deal with the problem, I typically push my chair back, stand up, and pace around. If I pass the kitchen, it may occur to me that I need a second cup of coffee. If I pass a window and see that it's a beautiful day, I'm likely to wonder if a long walk would give me the inspiration I need. If I pause next to the bookshelves, I'll probably notice that the books are totally out of order and thick with dust. How can I really expect myself to work well in such a discouraging setting?

If you've ever had a problem with procrastination, you can guess what happens next. I make coffee or take a walk or dust and reorganize the books. Then I drag myself back to my desk and discover that, for some reason, I'm still stuck in exactly the same place. The only differences are that it's an hour or two later and I'm that much more depressed over my lack of progress.

To avoid procrastinating, I could follow the example of a friend and make a poster that reads PUT OFF PROCRASTINATING. But it didn't help her much, and I doubt if it would work for me, either. I might even waste valuable work time staring at it and brooding over the fact that I don't have the strength of character to follow its advice!

Suppose instead that I set myself the concrete goal of doubling or tripling my average "time on task." If I usually manage to spend twenty minutes working between pauses, I'll try to push that to an hour. I know I won't reach my goal right away, but at least I'll be able to tell if I'm getting closer to it or not, or even, perhaps, farther away.

Achieving this goal may not *cure* my tendency to be too easily distracted, but it will certainly help. It will cut down on the amount of time I lose to distraction. It will give me more confidence in my own ability to set and reach goals. And as my habits change, *my goals will change, too.*

In the chapters that follow, you'll be introduced to some important motivational processes and learn how each of them can help or hurt your ability to get things done. I'll also give some examples of concrete, measurable goals that a person might choose to set, as a way of changing those motivational processes. Of course, these are just suggestions. There's nothing to stop you from coming up with ones that are better adapted to your particular situation.

Getting From Here To There

Once we've set a goal, we need to know what steps to take that will help us reach it. That's pretty obvious. What's not so obvious is that setting a goal and moving toward it are very different propositions. Simply deciding that you want to stop smoking does not tell you what's the best way to go about it. So what we need most is a map of psychological change with landmarks we can use to guide us in the right direction.

The Seven Steps

There are many ways of describing how people change, and as Rudyard Kipling said about the many ways of writing tribal ballads, "every single one of them is right." I find it helpful—and I hope you will, too—to think of the process of change in terms of these seven steps.

1. *Identify* an area in your life that you want to change.

2. *Explore* its frequency, meanings, and connections.

3. *Commit* yourself to change.

4. *Arrange* your surroundings to make change easier.

5. *Ask* for support from those close to you.

6. *Practice* putting the change into effect.

7. *Monitor* your progress.

Let's look closer at these steps.

Identify. The fact that you picked up this book shows that you've already started this process. You're concerned about the difficulties you've had in getting things done, and you are starting to suspect that the problem might be more one of motivation than of learning the "correct" techniques. But "motivation" is much too broad and shapeless a target.

Imagine that you've just witnessed a bank robbery and the police ask you to describe the robber. "Uh— it was a young guy in jeans and a dark jacket," you say.

That's a start, but it doesn't give the cops much to go on. They can't pull in every young man they see wearing jeans and a dark jacket.

At that point, an experienced officer will start asking you lots of questions. His goal is to narrow and sharpen your identification. What about hair color? eyes? race? facial hair? Did the thief wear glasses? have funny-shaped ears? Which hand did he hold the gun in? And so on, until you've given as detailed a description as you're capable of.

The process we're now involved in is a little like that. As you go on reading (and taking notes on the passages and ideas that ring a bell for you), your identification of what you think you need to work on will become sharper and clearer.

Don't worry if the identification isn't perfect, though. And you certainly shouldn't *wait* to get it perfect. You don't have to finish one step in order to start on the next. In fact, as we'll see, you'll probably come back to each of the steps more than once as you go along.

Explore. How central is the habit or pattern you hope to change? Is it something that you do often, or only from time to time? Does it seem to be linked to particular people or situations? What do they have in common?

Years ago, I moved to an apartment that had been vacant for several months. At the end of my first month there, I got an electric bill for several hundred dollars. I complained, of course, and explained. The service representative agreed that the bill was a mistake and told me to ignore it.

Two weeks later, I found a notice in the mail. My power was going to be turned off for nonpayment. I called again. I was told to ignore the notice. Two weeks after that, I got an even larger bill. Another phone call, another disconnect notice, another phone call—this went on for months. Finally I managed to speak to someone who straightened out the problem.

Every time I received one of those bills or disconnect notices, every time I reached for the phone to explain once again why the company's records were wrong, I was sure that my whole world was about to end. I knew the bill was a mistake, *they* knew it was a mistake, but that didn't matter one bit. The power company was going to seize my savings, throw me in debtor's prison, and never allow me to buy another watt of electricity as long as I lived.

Dozens of times, I came that close to writing a check for the amount they were demanding. *Anything* to get rid of the constant threat. The only reason I didn't was that I knew the check would bounce. But when it was all over, I realized that I had learned something valuable about myself.

Previously when I found myself in conflict with a large, powerful organization, I had instantly assumed that I couldn't possibly gain my point. "You can't fight City Hall." But in this case I noticed how little that belief had to do with reality. In fact, each time I called and explained, the person on the other end understood, agreed with me, and promised to help. And eventually I won my point.

I'll never know how many other times in my life I had *not* pressed a point—or not even noticed that I had a point to press—because I was so sure that it was no use. If I hadn't finally paid attention to my reactions and what they meant, however, I might never have noticed that basic assumption of helplessness and started working to change it.

You don't have to wait for a fight with the power company to start paying closer attention to your assumptions and reactions. You can begin right now. Start keeping a log.

Let's say that you've identified a pessimistic style as something you want to change. Each time you have to estimate your chances of success or failure at something, jot down the situation, your role in it, who else is involved, and what you expect the outcome to be. Go back later and compare what you expected to what actually happened. Look for common elements. Then, the next time one of those elements shows up, check your reactions. Are you making the same negative assumptions as last time?

Commit. The act of making a commitment to change is itself a powerful force for change. It's a way of applying pressure to ourselves in advance, *before* the pressure to break the commitment gets strong again. Once we've committed ourselves, we would feel weak or foolish if we went back on it.

Making a commitment can have a powerful effect even when the person didn't *choose* to make it. A famous experiment in social psychology illustrates this. Students were led to record speeches in favor of a new campus regulation that they didn't actually agree with. Then they found out that the speeches were going to be broadcast over the campus radio station. As a result, their opinions shifted in the direction of the regulation they had spoken against, in spite of their earlier doubts.

Commitments aren't everything, of course. Think of all the New Year's resolutions you've made and broken. Still, though most of us don't take New Year's resolutions very seriously and expect them to be broken, even they can have a big impact on how you lead your life.

Try this: next New Year's Eve, don't make a mental list of resolutions, *write it down.* Then take your list and tape it to your bathroom mirror. Or better still, post it someplace where everyone you're close to can read it. Do you still think you'll find it so easy to break those resolutions?

More generally, anything we can do to make it clear to ourselves and to others that the commitment is serious and important will make it that much easier to keep and harder to break. In some teen gangs, after a new member swears loyalty in front of all the others, he or she is tattooed on the face with the gang insignia. Talk about an obvious public commitment!

Don't worry—you don't have to go to such extremes to put the force of commitment to work for you. Once you've made a firm decision to change, *go public.* Tell others about your decision. If it's convenient, do it during a special occasion—your birthday party, an anniversary meal or, of course, on New Year's Eve. And if, now and then, you feel your commitment weakening, just remind yourself of the people who know about it and who'll notice whether you stick to it.

Arrange your surroundings. Set up cues that will

help and get rid of cues that will get in your way. When my neighbor, Carlo, first quit smoking, he went through his apartment, gathering up all the cigarettes and matches and tossing them in the garbage. Then he took all the ashtrays and put them away in a kitchen cabinet, on a very high shelf. Later, as his confidence grew, he brought the ashtrays out again, but only when he had visitors who smoked.

One way you can apply this idea to changing your motivational patterns is through the principle of *stimulus control*. A couple of years ago, we had friends from abroad visit us for a week. My office became a temporary guestroom, and I moved my desk and computer into the bedroom. Soon every time I ran into a minor hitch, I would get up from my desk and lie down on the bed—''just to think through the problem.'' I didn't get much work done that week, but I did accumulate a lot of quality nap time, because I couldn't associate my office with my bedroom as strongly as I associated my bedroom with sleep.

Try this the next time you start a major project, set aside a space that you can devote totally to that project. If it's your desk, clear it off. Move those piles of bills, catalogs, papers to be filed, books, and magazines somewhere else, anywhere else. Just get them *out of your sight* when you're at the desk. If you need to do something about them, get up and do it somewhere else. The same goes when you want a cup of coffee or a soda. Drink it somewhere else. For now, that space belongs to that project.

As you get used to the new arrangement, you'll find a marvelous increase in your ability to focus. It's not simply that you have fewer distractions. You're also beginning to associate being at the desk with one particular activity—working on your project.

Ask for support. You probably found this book in the section marked ''Self-Help,'' but ''self-help'' does not mean ''going it alone.'' It's pointless even to try. We all need caring, understanding support from those who are important to us. We especially need it when we're trying to break away from our old ways of doing things.

Getting help is easy. Just ask. Explain what you're trying to do and why you're trying to do it. You might even ask your friend or family member to read this book, or at least those parts that you think have the most to say about your situation.

The next step is give your helper something concrete to do. For example, if you are working on choosing tasks in a more realistic way, you might discuss particular situations as they come up. Get your helper's input on whether the choices you're making are realistic or not. If you're working on the ways you explain your successes and failures, talk about them. Does your helper agree that the task you just finished was very easy, and that that's why you were able to do it?

There's another way your helper can help, one that you may not have thought of. When you feel that you've accomplished something, made some movement in the direction you want, don't keep the good news to yourself. Let your helper help you celebrate.

Practice. We all know that learning to do something well requires practice. Once we reach a certain level, we also practice to stay there. Musicians and athletes think of practicing as almost a full-time job. Actors and elected officials rehearse before every important public appearance. Surgeons and pool players, choir members and sidewalk artists, all of them practice.

Practice is more than simple repetition. A house carpenter may drive thousands of nails every day, but he isn't *practicing* hitting nails on the head, he's just doing it. When I got my first computer, I also bought a program to teach me touch typing. I was tired of being the world's fastest one-finger typist. For a couple of months, I followed the program and I practiced. Then I quit. I had gotten as far as I felt I needed to. Since then, although I spend hours at the keyboard every day, I don't practice.

Here I'm using the word "practice" to mean not only doing something with the object of doing it a certain way, but paying closer attention to the way it's done than to the end result. When my daughter sits down at the piano and races through *Für Elise*, she thinks she's practicing. She isn't. If she were, she would pause after stumbling over a tricky passage. She would try it again and again, until her fingers moved through it easily.

Changing your motivational patterns involves systematic practice. Eventually, the new patterns will come to you as easily and spontaneously as the notes of *Für Elise* do to someone who has been teaching it to generations of ten-year-olds. But until then, you have to pay close attention to the process. You have to be willing to stop yourself in the middle and do it again.

When you have to try something new, do you usually assume that you'll screw up? The next time you're in that situation, practice some of the mental exercises that you'll learn later in the book. You may not feel any difference at first, but gradually your views of yourself and your ways of thinking about what you do will change. And as they change, so will the ways you act.

Monitor your progress. The log I suggested you start as a way of exploring the patterns you wanted to change, can have another use, too. As you start to practice new ways of motivating yourself, keep track of what you're doing and how it works.

Each time you find yourself in the kind of situation that gives you problems, write down a few words about it. What were your initial reactions? How did you try to apply the new motivational pattern? What was the result? Later on, in a quiet moment, look over your notes. Add any thoughts you have about what you might have done differently and (*very* important!) what you think you did right.

Gradually, this log will develop into a priceless database. You'll use it to look back on your progress. You'll see how far you've come and how you did it. You'll also notice areas that still need work, because the process is never really finished.

Here's a final thought about how we change. We'll take a closer look at what it means later on. For now, just read it over and think about it.

> *Live as if you are already*
> *the person you want to be.*

3

EXPECTING THE BEST AND THE WORST

Not long after I started teaching child psychology, I realized that I wanted to share my knowledge and ideas with a wider circle of people, especially parents. I decided that the best way to do that would be to write about the field for a popular audience.

One topic that seemed very important to me (and still does) was the ways children develop anxiety over achievement. So I wrote an article on the subject and sent it off to one of the most widely circulated magazines in the world.

A month or so later, the article came back. In a personal letter, the editor who had considered it told me that the topic was a little too narrow for their magazine. She went on to say that she would be happy to consider any other article ideas I might have.

I was too inexperienced, and too crushed by the rejection, to realize that this was an unusually *positive* response. The editor was actually encouraging me to write for them! But all I noticed was that they had turned down my article.

Years later, I don't know what I had expected or if I really believed I was going to sell my first article to one of the toughest markets around, but I do know this. After I got that rejection letter, I was sure that that magazine wouldn't be interested in anything I wrote. I never sent them anything else. As for the article that had been turned down, I stuffed it in a file drawer and eventually mislaid it.

Expectations and Actions

Whenever we decide to do something, whether it's going to the store for a quart of milk or making a major career change, we start off by making a mental plan. We don't necessarily know that that's what we've done, but if we stop and think, we can usually pinpoint at least some of the elements of the plan. These elements almost always include:

- a *goal*
- a *plan of action* to reach the goal
- an *expectation* of success or failure

Let's say I suddenly discover that, because of a mistake in subtraction, my rent check is about to bounce. That will mean paying a hefty service charge to the bank and another one to the landlord. I'll have a salary check to deposit at the end of the week, but what do I do now? I come up with a simple plan to deal with the problem. My *goal* is to have enough money in my account to cover the check. My *plan of action* is to ask a friend for a very short term loan. My *expectation* is that, when I do, he'll lend me the money and I'll put it in the bank, then pay him back at the end of the week.

So far, so good. But what if I say to myself, "My friend never has any spare cash," or, "He'll probably find some excuse to not lend me money." In that case, my expectation is that if I do ask him, I *won't* manage to raise the money I need. So why should I bother? It would be a total waste of time and effort, as well as a source of humiliation. I'll simply have to hope that the landlord is late in depositing my check.

Let's take a closer look at what just happened. I didn't ask for a loan because I expected that asking would not lead to my getting the loan. And because I didn't ask, I *won't* get the loan I need. In other words, based on my expectation, I acted in a way that made it more likely (in this case, certain) that my expectation would turn out to be right.

The name that's given to a sequence of events like this is a *self-fulfilling prophecy*. And once you begin to look for them, you'll start noticing them all around you.

- Dorie has heard about a hot new club that's supposed to be a lot of fun but really hard to get into. On Friday night, she and her friend, Les, decide to give it a try. They join the little crowd behind the rope. But they're so sure that they won't get picked that they hang around near the back of the crowd. The guy manning the door doesn't even see them. After twenty minutes, they leave, feeling bad.

- On the morning of his weekly tennis game with Phil, Randy wakes up feeling terrific. He is sure that he's going to win for a change. This confidence leads him to play a stronger, more aggressive game than usual. Phil, taken by surprise, is a little thrown off and plays less well than usual. Randy wins.

- When his company is taken over, Sy is convinced that his new boss will ax him and put one of her own people in his place. He goes into his first evaluation conference with such a chip on his shoulder that his boss decides she can't work with him. A few weeks later, Sy is transferred to a lower level job in another division.

And, there's what happened to me when I tried to write about children's achievements and anxieties. When my first article was rejected, I came to expect that anything else I did in that direction would be rejected, too, so I didn't try again.

I'm not saying that, if I *had* tried, I would have been wildly successful. I might not have gotten anywhere. I'll never know. But because I expected failure, I acted in a way that *guaranteed* failure. And that's a pity.

Tripping Yourself Up

Are you being hobbled by the effects of your own expectations? We'll look at ways to get a more detailed answer to that question later. For now, just read over the following everyday situations, then respond to the questions after each one. Don't take too long over it or think too hard about your answers. Your first response is probably the most accurate one. And for goodness' sake, don't worry about giving the "right" answer. No one is looking over your shoulder.

* * *

You got your ten-year-old a multimedia computer for Christmas. She's having a great time with it, writing school reports, painting fantasy landscapes, and chasing Carmen Sandiego all over the globe. She asks you to help her with one of her paintings. You sit down at the computer and see rows of incomprehensible icons down one side of the screen and across the bottom. You click on one and try to use the mouse to draw a circle. For some reason, you get a purple diamond instead.

How likely is it that you will:

1. decide that you simply are not part of the Computer Generation and tell your kid to ask one of her schoolmates for help?
   - ❏ very unlikely
   - ☑ fairly unlikely
   - ❏ fairly likely
   - ❏ very likely

2. decide to try clicking on some more of the buttons, until something reasonable happens?
   - ❏ very unlikely
   - ❏ fairly unlikely
   - ❏ fairly likely
   - ☑ very likely

3. decide that the painting program was probably designed with ordinary people in mind and ask your kid if she knows where the user's manual is?
   - ❏ very unlikely
   - ☑ fairly likely
   - ❏ fairly unlikely
   - ❏ very likely

4. fling your hands in the air and say that the program was obviously designed by a bunch of idiots?
   - ☑ very unlikely
   - ❏ fairly unlikely
   - ❏ fairly likely
   - ❏ very likely

At a friend's party, you get into a conversation with someone who seems interesting and likable. Before leaving, you exchange names and telephone numbers. *How likely is it that you will:*

1. stay in touch with the person and eventually become friends?
   - ❑ very unlikely
   - ☑ fairly unlikely
   - ❑ fairly likely
   - ❑ very likely

2. wait to see if the other person calls you?
   - ❑ very unlikely
   - ❑ fairly unlikely
   - ☑ fairly likely
   - ❑ very likely

3. call once, and if it doesn't work out that time, not call again?
   - ❑ very unlikely
   - ❑ fairly unlikely
   - ☑ fairly likely
   - ❑ very likely

4. keep calling until you get through?
   - ☑ very unlikely
   - ❑ fairly unlikely
   - ❑ fairly likely
   - ❑ very likely

Your department head calls a meeting to talk over a problem that the company is facing. At one point in the discussion, you have an idea for a new approach to dealing with the problem. When you mention it, your department head says it sounds interesting but then moves on to something else. Your idea doesn't come up again during the rest of the meeting. *How likely is it that you will:*

1. drop the idea, since apparently no one thinks it has any promise?
   - ❑ very unlikely
   - ❑ fairly unlikely
   - ☑ fairly likely
   - ❑ very likely

2. ask your superior if you can explore the idea further on your own?
   - ❑ very unlikely
   - ☑ fairly unlikely
   - ❑ fairly likely
   - ❑ very likely

3. develop the idea in more detail and submit it to your boss in the form of a memo?
   - ❑ very unlikely
   - ☑ fairly unlikely
   - ❑ fairly likely
   - ❑ very likely

A friend tells you about an evening course on how to watch films. You love films, and you've always wanted to find out more about what to look for when you go to see one. But when you read over the brochure for the course, you find that it's full of terms like "semiotics," "deconstruction," and "postmodern sensibility."

How likely is it that you will:

1. sign up for the course, then at the first session ask the instructor to give you the name of a book that explains any concepts that are new to you?
   - ☑ very unlikely
   - ❑ fairly unlikely
   - ❑ fairly likely
   - ❑ very likely

2. decide that all this trendy stuff is way beyond you and that you can probably learn more by staying home and watching The Movie Channel?
   - ❑ very unlikely
   - ❑ fairly unlikely
   - ❑ fairly likely
   - ☑ very likely

3. go to the first session, decide that it's over your head, and drop out?
   - ❑ very unlikely
   - ❑ fairly unlikely
   - ☑ fairly likely
   - ❑ very likely

As you look over your responses to these four situations, there's something important to notice. There's a strong chance that *all* of the reactions described will turn out to be self-fulfilling prophecies.

The negative expectations almost certainly will. If you decide that you can't understand that new software or the course on film, you *won't*. And if you don't follow through on your idea for dealing with your company's problem, who is going to push you to?

On the other hand, the more optimistic responses are likely to become self-fulfilling, too. You can probably learn to use that paint program, if you assume that you can and you put in the necessary effort. If you believe that you and the person you met at that party can become friends, and you act on that belief, chances are that you'll turn out to be right.

Teachers and Expectations

Self-fulfilling prophecies aren't always something we make about ourselves. Others can make them about us, too—especially people that have some kind of influence over us. One striking example is teachers and their pupils.

In the mid-1960s, Harvard psychologist Robert Rosenthal and his co-worker, Lenore Jacobson, went to an elementary school in California and gave an IQ test to students in the first through sixth grades. Later, every teacher in the school was given the names of five students in his or her class who, according to the test results, were likely to be ''rapid bloomers'' and show sudden spurts of intellectual growth.

In fact, these kids were no different from their classmates. Rosenthal and Jacobson had picked their names at random from the class rosters. But when the children were retested at the end of the school year, the supposed rapid bloomers showed greater gains than the other students. Their teachers' expectations for them had apparently increased the kids' scores on the IQ test.

Rosenthal and Jacobson called this the "Pygmalion effect," after the legend of the sculptor who fell in love with the statue he had carved. Their findings later came under a lot of fire, for fairly technical reasons. But the basic conclusion, that what teachers expect of their students affects how the students perform, is rock solid.

The younger sibling's burden. If you had an older brother or sister who went through the same elementary school ahead of you and had some of the same teachers, you already know firsthand what we mean when we talk about teacher expectations. If your older sibling was a top student, everybody expected you to live up to that. And if he or she was a poor student, or worse, a troublemaker, you had major problems ahead of you.

Researcher Burleigh Seaver studied the records of all the older/younger pairs of siblings in two elementary schools in a Chicago suburb. He looked at the grades and Stanford Achievement Test scores of the younger kids, comparing those who had the *same* first grade teacher as their older sibling with those who had a *different* first grade teacher.

The results were a little complicated but very clear. If the older brother or sister had been a good student, the younger kids who had the same teacher did better than those who had a different teacher. But when the older brother or sister had been a poor student, the ones with the same teacher did *worse* than the ones with a different teacher. And we're not just talking about their report cards, which could have been affected by prejudice. The same differences showed up on the kids' standardized test scores.

Taking in expectations. How did the teachers' expectations get translated into the children's test results? There are a few different factors at work. First, teachers give more encouragement in class to students they expect to do well. Even when a low-expectation student does do well, the way the teacher praises him or her is likely to be subtly different.

Something else probably has an even deeper, more lasting effect. Children notice when someone expects them to succeed or fail. If that someone is an important adult, such as a teacher, the kids often take in the expectation and make it their own. They come to believe it, and to act in ways that help make it come true.

Did you ever have a teacher who somehow let you know, without ever saying it out loud, that you were hopeless at something? I still remember Mrs. Norman's fourth grade class and our weekly art lessons. I had a lot of fun drawing and coloring, but my trees always came out looking like green lollipops on brown sticks. Mrs. Norman knew that children with even the slightest artistic ability drew trees that looked like trees. I'd never heard of Matisse or Picasso, never mind Derain, and I wasn't in a position to argue.

It didn't help that Edith, the daughter of an architect, sat in front of me. *Her* trees looked real enough to attract a nearsighted sparrow, and her fashion drawings could have been traced from a magazine ad. (I had mean-spirited moments when I was sure they

were.) Mrs. Norman hovered over Edith for most of
the period, making encouraging noises in her throat.
Then at the end of the period, she would start hovering over me, making impatient noises.

I got the message. I still think I might like to take
a painting class one of these days, when I have time.
Then I remember those trees like green lollipops, and
I wonder if I'll ever find the time—or the heart.

"Day By Day, In Every Way . . ."

In the early 1920s, a former druggist from Nancy,
France, toured the United States to spread the word
about a new, supposedly scientific way to achieve
health and happiness. His name was Emile Coué, and
he called his method *auto-suggestion*.

Coué's tour was front-page news. At crowded
meetings in major cities around the country, he told
his listeners exactly what to do. Every morning, they
were to stand in front of the mirror and say, out loud,
the words, *Every day, in every way, I am getting better and better*. Repeated thirty times a day, with sin-
cerity, this was said to cure serious health problems,
get rid of varicose veins, and even restore hair to bald
heads.

You may think—as I do—that Coué's particular
brand of snake-oil sounds really silly. Maybe so, but
at the time, a lot of prominent people, including Henry
Ford and the president of the Museum of Natural History, said how impressed they were with it. People
flocked to Coué's lectures and signed up for lessons
at the Coué Institutes that sprang up around the country.

Then, after a couple of years, the Coué Method was dead, the victim died of the same disease that kills most faddish "cures." When it didn't produce the miracles its promoters promised, people got disillusioned with it and moved on to something else.

The reason I'm telling you about Coué and his "Method" is that I want to be sure no one thinks that this book is suggesting a similar brand of miracle cure. Remember:

> If you don't have any influence over the result, your expectations, positive or negative, won't make a bit of difference.

I can tell myself as often as I like that my Lotto ticket is going to win the $23 million jackpot. I might even manage to talk myself into thinking that I believe it. No matter—the odds against me will still be just the same as if I were sure I was going to lose.

The same, unfortunately, is true for baldness. Try as I may (and believe me, I'm willing), no amount of confidence or auto-suggestion is going to put a fresh crop of hair on my pate.

So having more positive expectations won't cure baldness. And it won't keep floodwaters from carrying your house downstream, either. But if we're talking about situations in which what we think, feel, and do *does* have an impact on the outcome, those who have more positive expectations come out way ahead.

Bad things can happen to anyone. The company you work for goes belly-up, you slip on a patch of ice and break your hip, your oldest friend dies in a car crash—having positive expectations won't keep bad things from happening. What it will do, however, is help you ride with the punches more easily and bounce back faster. And when the possibility of *good* things comes along, it's the person with more positive expectations who is likely to notice and take advantage of the opportunity.

As Martin Seligman points out in his book, *Learned Optimism*, optimists achieve more at work, at school, and in their personal lives. Others are more likely to choose them as leaders. They are healthier and happier, and they may even live longer. That's quite a list of benefits, and it's only a quick summary. Positive expectations aren't the only ingredient in what Seligman means by "optimism," but they are fundamental.

Assessing Your Expectations

Before we go on to look at ways to change our expectations, it's important to have a clear idea of where we're starting from, what psychologists call a *baseline*.

Here's how to find your baseline: over the next two or three days, whenever you're going to embark on some activity in which your actions affect the outcome, first take a few moments to complete the following sentences:

I am about to:

The *best* reasonably likely outcome is:

The *worst* reasonably likely outcome is:

The outcome I expect is:

    (*put a mark somewhere along the line*)

worst   best

Later, *after* you've done whatever it is, answer one more question:

The *actual* outcome was:

←――――――――――――――――――――――――――→
worst   best

Here's an example of how to do this self-assessment.

I am going to: try out that new recipe for chicken ragoût when our friends come over for dinner tomorrow night.

The *best* reasonably likely outcome is: everyone will love it, the kitchen won't be too much of a mess, I won't have spent a fortune on materials, and there'll be enough left over for lunch the next day.

The *worst* reasonably likely outcome is: it'll be completely inedible, my friends will make fun of me, we'll have to call out for pizza, and I'll be in a foul mood all evening.

The outcome I expect is:

              X
←――――――――――――――――――――――――――→
worst   best

(That is, I think it'll be okay, but I'm far from sure.)

[Afterward]

The *actual* outcome was:

X

← worst _____ best →

(In fact, it turned out pretty well.)

Okay, now it's your turn. Over the next couple of days, find the time to fill out the following pages. Try, if possible, to write about at least one situation that's work-related and one that concerns your personal life.

I am about to:

The *best* reasonably likely outcome is:

The *worst* reasonably likely outcome is:

The outcome I expect is:

←————————————————————————————→

worst   best

[Afterward]

The *actual* outcome was:

←————————————————————————————→

worst   best

I am about to:

The *best* reasonably likely outcome is:

The *worst* reasonably likely outcome is:

The outcome I expect is:

worst   best

[Afterward]
The *actual* outcome was:

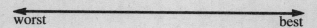

worst   best

I am about to:

The *best* reasonably likely outcome is:

The *worst* reasonably likely outcome is:

The outcome I expect is:

⟵─────────────────────────────────⟶
worst   best

[Afterward]
The *actual* outcome was:

⟵─────────────────────────────────⟶
worst   best

I am about to:

The *best* reasonably likely outcome is:

The *worst* reasonably likely outcome is:

The outcome I expect is:

worst ←————————————————————————→ best

[Afterward]
The *actual* outcome was:

worst ←————————————————————————→ best

In psychological research, data collection and data analysis are two separate stages. Now that you've collected the data, here is how to analyze it.

First, read over your best-case and worst-case descriptions. Which ones are more vivid? People with lowered expectations generally find it easier to think of all the bad things that might happen than to imagine what a really positive outcome might look like.

Imagine that you're someone else, reading what you wrote. Which descriptions do you think you'd find more realistic or convincing? That's a hard judgment to make, of course. You wrote them, so you're bound to think they're all just fine. But if you look them over with a stranger's eye, you may notice some odd features.

Remember the one I filled out, about trying a new recipe? Take another look. Do you really think it's likely that my guests would make fun of me because something I cooked didn't work? They might roll their eyes a little, when they thought I wasn't looking, but surely that's as far as they'd go. (If not, maybe I need new friends.) In other words, my fears were exaggerated. That's another symptom of lowered expectations.

Now look at how you marked the two scales. What you want to examine isn't so much where you put your checkmarks on each of the scales as the relationship between the two. Where was your expectation (the *before* scale) in relation to your outcome (the *after* scale)? Were both more or less in the middle? Were your expectations consistently lower (nearer the "worst" end) than your outcomes? Or (this isn't unusual, either) did you expect negative outcomes and then afterwards decide that that's exactly what you'd gotten? Or expect negative outcomes, because that way you wouldn't be disappointed, whatever happened?

Changing Your Expectations

Can we change our expectations? Can we learn to overcome all the negative, pessimistic attitudes that we've inherited from our pasts? I'm persuaded that the answer is "Yes." Not that it's easy. After all, it's a big change in the way we regard and approach the world. There's always the possibility of slipping back to our old habits, too. But it can be done. The techniques exist, and they can be put to use by anybody who decides to do so.

Before we start, however, we'd better remember that there's a big difference between making short-term and long-term changes in our expectations. One is like holding a personal pep rally. The other requires working on our thinking patterns.

Do you remember the scene early in *The Sound of Music* when the young Maria, fresh from the convent, goes off to her first job as governess to the von Trapp children? As she walks along, she buoys up her spirits with a cheerful, bouncy song that proclaims, "I have confidence in me!" Then she arrives at the gates of the von Trapp estate, takes one look at the imposing mansion, and whispers, "Oh, Heavens!" All her new confidence evaporates on the spot.

A team that gathers in the locker room before a big game and chants, "We're gonna win! We're gonna win!" may go out pumped up enough to play with more energy. That extra energy may even make a difference in the outcome of the game. But if the game starts to go against them, their temporary expectation of winning will disappear as quickly as it appeared. They'll be back where they started—or a little behind where they started.

Three Distortions

What accounts for unrealistically low expectations, the sort that turn into self-fulfilling prophecies? We'll be looking at some of the underlying factors in chapters to come. For now, consider the idea that we're dealing with at least three related kinds of mental distortion:

- *distorted recollections*. You find it easier to *remember* past failures than past successes.

- *distorted perceptions*. You're more likely to *notice* the factors that would make for failure than those that would make for success.

- *distorted reflections*. You give *greater weight* to factors that predict failure than to those that predict success.

To set in motion a process that will make long-term changes in our expectations, we have to learn to counter all three of these tendencies to distort. One way to do this is to use a *clarification worksheet*. Let's say you're considering a new project and you're inclined not to do it because you don't think it will work out. Try completing a worksheet like this:

If I:

The outcome will probably be:

Because in the past:

And because: 1.

2.

3.

4.

This may be persuasive, but there's also another important step, arguing with yourself.

Draw a line under what you've written so far. Write in big letters, "ON THE OTHER HAND." Then cast your mind over the past until you find a positive experience that contradicts the negative one. You don't have to get your mental scales to balance exactly, as long as you have recollections on both sides.

Now, for each of the reasons you gave to expect a negative outcome, find one that would lead you to expect a positive outcome. Once again, don't expect them to balance each other exactly. What counts is gradually realizing that there are as many possible arguments on one side as on the other.

Once you have your new list, imagine two lawyers engaged in a court case. One of you is defending the original expectation of failure. The other is arguing that that expectation is not supported by the evidence. It's a matter of professional ethics that each side does its best to win the argument.

At first, it's likely that the low expectation side will be stronger. You're more familiar—even more comfortable—with it, after all. In a way, that doesn't much matter. What does count is that we're bringing our expectations into the daylight, where we see them as they are.

Still more important, we're making those expectations, as well as the distorted assumptions that help create them, more and more open to question. We're training ourselves to notice all the reasons that we *should* expect to succeed and to give those reasons the weight they deserve. Gradually, from knowing that we *ought to* have higher expectations, we reach the point of realizing that we *do* have them. And just as expectations of failure can become self-fulfilling prophecies, so can expectations of success.

> *What we expect shapes what we do.*
> *What we do shapes how well we do.*
> *How well we do shapes what we expect.*

4

MOTIVES AND GOALS

To introduce the ideas we'll be talking about in this chapter, I'd like to give you a couple of exercises to do. If you don't want to do the exercises just now, or if you don't have the time, please do *not* skip ahead in the chapter. If you already knew what the point of the exercises was, that might lead you to do them the way you think you *should* do them, and that would take away a lot of their value to you.

The first exercise involves visualization. You'll need up to half an hour to do it properly, so wait until you have the time free. Then take some paper, a pencil or pen, and a watch, and sit down in a quiet place.

First read over the following questions and take ten minutes to think about them. Then spend up to another twenty minutes writing your answers to them. Don't worry about grammar, spelling, or organization. Just get your thoughts down as completely and in as much detail as you can.

1. What specific goal do you want to achieve in the next year?

2. What specific steps do you mean to take to get to that goal?

3. What obstacles within yourself do you think you'll have to overcome to reach your goal?

4. What outside obstacles do you think you'll have to overcome to reach your goal?

5. How do you think you'll feel if you reach your goal?

6. How do you think you'll feel if you *fail* to reach your goal?

7. Where will you turn for help in reaching your goal?

8. How strongly do you want to reach this goal?

9. How important is this goal to you, compared to other things you want out of life?

Now put your answers away, someplace where you're sure you can find them. You'll want to come back to them later.

Toss the Paper

After all that thinking and writing you just did, you probably need to stand up and stretch. Here's another exercise that will let you do just that. You'll need half a dozen sheets of paper, a wastebasket, and some masking tape.

Crumple the sheets of paper into balls, not too tight, not too loose, and place the wastebasket at one end of a room. With short strips of masking tape, make marks on the floor at one foot, two feet, three feet,

PAPER TOSS RECORD SHEET

THROW#	LINE#	HIT?(✓)
1		
2		
3		
4		
5		
6		
7		
8		
9		
10		
11		
12		
13		
14		
15		
16		
17		
18		
19		
20		

and so on, from the basket. The farthest should be ten or twelve feet from the basket.

The object of this game is to toss the paper balls, one by one, into the wastebasket. You should take twenty shots at it. On each toss, you may stand as close or as far as you like from the basket. Use the score sheet on the previous page to keep track of how you do. On each throw, simply jot down the number of the line you stand at, then make a check mark if the ball goes in.

When you've made all twenty tries, save the paper balls. You'll be using them again.

Goals and Motives

Alan learned to ski fairly well in college, when he was dating a woman who was an avid skier. After he stopped seeing her, he stopped skiing, too. Last summer, he was transferred from Utah to his company's home office in suburban Connecticut. It hasn't been easy, living in a new area where he didn't know anyone. A few weeks ago, however, some co-workers invited him to join them over a holiday weekend at a ski house they'd rented in Vermont. Of course he said yes.

When they got to the ski area on Saturday morning, Alan went right to the beginners' slope. It was really easy. He was so comfortable that he felt like spending the whole weekend there. After a few runs, however, he noticed that he was skiing several notches better than anyone else on the baby slope. Not that that bothered him particularly, but he couldn't help wondering what his friends would think if they saw him.

Suddenly self-conscious, he caught a gondola that took him to the middle of the mountain, then changed to another that went practically to the top. Then he studied the big map on the wall of the warming hut. All the trails down were labeled Expert. He chose one at random and started down.

"Down" was the word, all right. After falling for the fifth time in fifty yards, Alan took off his skis and walked the rest of the way to the mid-mountain transfer point. After a moment's hesitation, he boarded the gondola to the top again and tried another of the Expert trails. It was no easier than the first.

By midafternoon, he had tried four different Expert trails, with the same results each time. Bruised and worn out, he made his way down to the base lodge. He was determined to find some excuse to stay off the slopes for the rest of the weekend and even more determined not to let anyone talk him into going skiing again.

The two exercises you just did and Alan's disastrous ski weekend are all about choosing goals: What you do when you face a range of tasks with different levels of difficulty and probability of success, and how you decide which one to do.

Any good-size ski area has slopes and trails for people at every skill level. It's a simple matter of sound business sense. Alan was certainly a good enough skier to manage the novice slopes. He might even have been able to handle one of the less demanding of the intermediate slopes. But he didn't choose those. First he headed for the easiest slope he could find. Then he switched to the hardest.

Why he did this has to do with his *achievement motivation*. The theory of achievement motivation was developed mainly by Professors David Mc-Clelland of Harvard and John Atkinson of the University of Michigan. It says that which goals we choose is strongly influenced by two separate motives: the *motive to succeed* and the *motive to avoid failure*. Before we examine these particular motives, though, we ought to understand motives in general and how they work.

Usually, when we talk about motives, we're asking why someone did something, that is: what was the need or emotion or desire behind their action? And we're most likely to ask the question when the action itself is at least a little out of the ordinary.

Take mystery stories, for example. The crime breaks the ordinary pattern of day-to-day life. To unmask the villain, the detective tries to figure out the motive. What pushed the criminal to commit the crime: jealousy, rage, passion, greed, fear of being caught? The list can be as long as the author's imagination and knowledge of human nature make it.

Because the action itself is out of the ordinary, the motive often turns out to be very specific to the situation. A crooked bank teller sets a fire to destroy the evidence of his embezzlements. A former movie star murders the plastic surgeon who ruined her face and career.

It's that way outside of novels, too. You arrive at work and say, "Good morning," to a co-worker in the hallway. He nods and waves. You probably don't give his motive a second thought. But suppose that, instead, he scowls at you and growls, "What's so good about it?" Unless he's notorious for imitating

Oscar the Grouch, you're likely to wonder what made him act that way on this particular occasion.

Motives Are Stable, Long-Term Needs

Psychologists like McClelland and Atkinson use the word *motive* in a rather different way. First, they see motives as stable. If you have a high motive to succeed today, you probably had one last year and five years before that. Unless something peculiar happens, you'll still have it five years from now.

Second, a person's motives affect what he or she does across a wide range of situations. For example, someone with a strong friendship (''affiliation'') motive will be on the lookout for chances to make friends on the job, on vacation, at home, and even on the bus. In this sense, motives go a long way toward describing how one individual is psychologically different from another.

Third, it's helpful to think of a motive as being a long-term psychological *need*. So the hunger motive is a need for the satisfaction that comes from food. The friendship motive is a need for the positive feeling that comes from being liked. The security motive is a need to *avoid* the negative feeling of being threatened by something.

The Two Achievement Motives

What kind of sense does it make to talk, as Atkinson and McClelland do, about a motive to succeed and a different motive to avoid failure? Don't succeeding and avoiding failure amount to the same thing? No, not if you think about these two motives as being needs.

Looked at that way, the motive to succeed is a need for the positive feeling—*pride* or a feeling of *accomplishment*—that comes with success. The motive to avoid failure is a need to avoid the negative feeling—*shame* or a feeling of *incompetence*—that comes with failure. And wanting to get pride is not at all the same thing as wanting to avoid shame.

Suppose you're at a friend's house. Maybe the two of you are going to a movie and your friend is running a little late. While you're waiting, you notice a puzzle on the table, one of those square plastic gizmos where you have to slide the little pieces around until the numbers on them are in the right order. Do you pick it up and start fiddling with it? Or do you start glancing through a magazine instead?

You may say that it all depends whether you like puzzles or not. And that's true, up to a point. But your achievement motives come into it, too.

If you have a strong need to get feelings of pride from success, you'll be inclined to try something that offers you a chance to get those feelings. Solving a puzzle may not be on a level with clinching a big sale or developing a new miracle drug, but it *is* an accomplishment.

On the other hand, if you start working on it, there's always the possibility that you might fail. Based on my own experience with those puzzles, I'd have to say it's a very strong possibility. So if you're most concerned with avoiding the bad feelings that you get from failure, you may not take that risk. The very best way to avoid failure, after all, is to stay away from *anything* you might fail at.

Achievement Motives and Incentives

We all know what incentives are. Fill up your tank and get a free set of glasses. Take out a home equity loan and get a toaster oven. Lead your region in sales and get a boat trip down the Rhine. Be at the *bottom* of your region in sales and get a pink slip, suitable for framing.

The formula is simple—do something, get something.

In the real world, there are lots of different incentives for success. Some—fame, money, admiration—come from outside, and others, such as the pride we feel when we accomplish something, come from within. There are lots of negative incentives for failure, too, including poverty, scorn and contempt from other people, and worse, self-hatred and self-contempt.

Have you ever done something that was profitable but that left you feeling personally dissatisfied? Or something that you felt proud of but that didn't bring much in the way of financial rewards? Then you already know about the difference between internal and external incentives. Odd as it may sound, achievement motivation theory is not so concerned with the effects of incentives from outside. What it mainly deals with instead are the *psychological* incentives that are linked to success and failure and the ways that they affect what we do.

The Risks We Choose

Imagine that you're about to play a computer game. You have to select what level of difficulty you want.

You're not going to win or lose any prizes, and you're not competing against anyone else. All that's at stake are whatever good feelings you'll get from success and whatever bad feelings you'll get from failure. What level of difficulty do you choose?

If you have a lot of the motive to succeed, your main concern is to get the good feelings that come with success. You might think that you'd choose the easiest level which would guarantee success, but you probably won't feel much pride when you succeed at something very easy. So you might choose the hardest level. Success there will certainly give you lot of pride, but look how unlikely it is that you *will* succeed. So that doesn't turn out to be a great choice, either. Look what happens, however, if you decide to try a *fairly challenging* level of difficulty—somewhere between too hard for you and too easy. You'll have a pretty good chance of succeeding *and* you'll feel pretty good about it when you do.

If you're someone who's more worried about avoiding the bad feelings you'd get from failure, one way to avoid them is to choose an easy level. You're not likely to fail then. But there's another way, too. You can choose a very *hard* level. That makes it practically certain that you'll fail, but how bad do you have to feel about it?

The way Alan, our skier, acted was typical of people who have a high motive to avoid failure. His first impulse was to hang out on the baby slope, where he was sure to do well. Then he began to think that others might think it looked funny. So he switched to trails that were too hard for him. He fell time after time, and he didn't have any of the fun he might have had skiing on easier slopes. But it wasn't his fault; the trails were too hard. And he could tell himself that he had shown high aspirations, and courage, and persistence.

Assess Yourself

It's time to take a close look at your score sheet from the paper toss game, back on page 69. What's most revealing about this game is the *pattern* of your choices. Where did you start? Near? Far? In the middle somewhere? When you missed a throw, where did you stand the next time? How about when you *made* a throw?

Take a look at the following sample score sheets. The numbers show which line each person stood at for each throw. A plus sign next to the number means that the paper ball went into the basket on that throw.

What do you notice about the patterns? Which players are most alike? Your first impulse might be to say that Martin and Jessica are alike, because they both started pretty far from the basket, and Joel and Laura are alike because they both started fairly close. But look what happened after the first two or three throws.

Joel and Jessica show the same behavior. When they scored, they moved farther back. When they didn't score, they moved closer. But Martin stayed far from the basket even when his throws kept missing. And Laura glued herself to the neighborhood of the target, even when almost every toss went in.

The way Jessica and Joel acted suggests that they were mainly interested in the pride that comes with success. Jessica is obviously a better thrower than Joel. That's why her score is higher. But that doesn't

THROW	MARTIN	JOEL	JESSICA	LAURA
1	8	+3	8	+3
2	9	+3	8	+3
3	9	+4	7	3
4	+9	4	+7	+2
5	10	+4	8	+2
6	10	6	+8	2
7	10	6	8	+1
8	10	6	+7	+2
9	11	5	8	3
10	9	+5	+8	+3
11	+8	+5	8	+2
12	10	+6	7	+2
13	11	7	+7	2
14	+10	6	+8	+2
15	12	+6	8	+2
16	12	6	+8	+2
17	12	7	9	2
18	12	+7	9	+1
19	12	7	+9	+1
20	12	6	10	+1
TOTAL SCORE	27	43	53	29

really matter. Both of them were doing the same thing. They kept trying different distances, in search of one that would be challenging enough but not *too* difficult.

As for the other two, picture Martin, all the way across the room, hurling those paper balls. Yes, almost all of them miss, but this is obviously a guy who dreams the impossible dream! And Laura is smart enough to have psyched out the game. She doesn't even have to throw the paper balls. She simply leans over and *drops* them in. But after what we've learned about achievement motivation, we have good reason to think that, whether they know it or not, both of them are basically acting out of fear of failure.

Now take another look at your own score sheet. Try to pretend that it belongs to a stranger. Which of the four we just studied is it most like? Are you a Martin, a Joel, a Jessica, or a Laura?

Telling Stories About Achievement

Another way to assess people's motivation is to look at the themes that show up in stories they write. This method has been used ever since the 1930s. The underlying idea is very simple. If people are very hungry, food and eating will show up in their stories. If they are concerned about getting and keeping friends, they'll write stories around that theme. And if high achievement is what they're most concerned about, *that* will show up. Then it becomes a matter of figuring out how to spot it.

Try your hand. Here are two stories, both written on the topic of, "A student sitting at a desk at home."

A. Jim is studying for a big exam tomorrow. He was out with flu for over a week, and he's way behind. He borrowed a friend's notes, but he's not sure he understands them. He looks at the clock and wishes he could have gone to a movie with his girlfriend, but the studying is more important. He's thinking that he'll need an awful lot of good luck to get a decent mark. He wishes the exam wasn't until next week, so he'd have more time to learn the material. He goes in and manages to do okay. In fact, with the curve he even ends up with an A.

B. Frank is studying for a big exam tomorrow. The course is important to him, because he needs it to get into med school. He was out with flu for over a week, so he's way behind. He borrowed a friend's notes and spent time talking them over with him, and now he's trying to fit everything he learned together. He wants to get a higher score than on the last exam and bring up his average. He thinks if he studies harder, he'll do well in spite of being out. Thanks to his hard work, he gets the second highest score in the class and finishes the semester with an A.

What do you notice about these two stories? There are a lot of similarities between them. Both students are getting ready for an important exam. Both missed school and are trying to make up for it by using a friend's notes. Both are thinking about how they'll do on the exam, and both end up getting A's.

But now look at the differences. Jim is concerned

mostly about getting by. And in the end, that's just what he does. He gets an A, it's true. But that has more to do with how the other students in the class did ("the curve") than with his own performance. He would have been happy just to do okay.

Frank, on the other hand, is very clear that he wants to do well. In fact, he's determined to improve on his last exam. He sees the course as important to a long term goal (med school) and thanks to hard work, he turns in an exceptional performance. An expert at scoring the themes in stories of this sort would say that the person who wrote the story about Frank shows all the signs of a high motive to succeed. The person who wrote Story A, shows few, if any.

Raising Your Achievement Motivation

If you're starting to suspect that you must be higher in fear of failure than in the motive to succeed, there is something you can do about it.

The program that follows makes use of a very simple but very powerful psychological process. If you systematically practice thinking, feeling, and acting like a person with high achievement motivation, gradually *you become such a person*.

In effect, what you will be doing is taking apart that old web of habitual responses that don't work for you. At the same time, you will start putting in place a new network of thoughts, feelings, and ways of acting. This new network will be more positive and more productive and will help you feel better about yourself and your achievements.

One caution: this program will work, but only if

you really commit yourself to follow it. If all you do
is look through it and say to yourself, "That sounds
like a good idea," it won't do you much good. You
might as well read the label of a bottle of aspirin and
expect your headache to go away.

Refine and Redefine Your Goals

Remember the goal statement you wrote at the beginning of this chapter? (You *did* write it, didn't you?
If not, take the time right now to do it.) Find it and
read it over.

Let's concentrate on your answer to Question One,
the specific goal you want to get done in the next year.

- What *sort* of goal is it? One that mainly involves your career? Your personal life? A social, or financial, or family, or spiritual goal?
- How *specific* is it? When you get to the end
  of they year, will you have any way of telling
  how close you've come to accomplishing it?
- How *achievement-related* is it? Will you judge
  what you've done against some standard of
  excellence?

If you're like most people, you'll find that your first
try at a goal statement is a long way from being specific enough. For example,

- "I want to get my life organized."
- "I want to spend more time with my family."
- "I want to move ahead faster in my career."

- "I want to get more fun out of life."
- "I want to feel more at peace with myself."

I'm not saying that any of these is a *bad* goal to have, but they're not very useful. They are much too general and don't suggest any practical steps to achieve them. Worse, even if you do manage to take some steps toward them, they don't offer you any way to have a clear sense of progress.

By way of comparison, look at these goal statements.

- "I want to learn to Rollerblade well."
- "I want to organize my work week in a way that will leave my weekends free to be with my family."
- "I want to increase my sales and commission income by fifteen percent."
- "I want to save at least one-quarter of what we'll need for the down payment on a house."
- "I want to start my own business at least part-time."

Do you see how these goal statements make it possible to give real, concrete answers to the second question, about the specific steps you mean to take to get to your goal? Whether it's taking Rollerblade lessons or attending a small-business exposition, you'll know as you do it that you are moving, no matter how slowly or quickly, in the direction you want to go.

Notice that, however worthwhile *and* specific these goal statements are, only some of them are really achievement-related. Learning to Rollerblade well is, because you'll judge how well you're doing by looking at others who know how to Rollerblade. That is, you're comparing what you've done against a standard of excellence. The same is true of increasing your sales or starting your own business. But saving for a house or freeing more time to be with your family, important as they may be in your scale of values, are *not* achievement-related.

Now sit down and write another goal statement, responding to each of the questions on pages 67 and 68. This time, be sure that your goal is *specific*, that it can be *evaluated*, and that you will judge how well you do in achieving it according to some standard of excellence. You should start seeing a difference already.

Think Like a Motivated Person

A few pages back, we saw how someone's concerns can show up in the stories they write. We also saw that what looks like an expression of the motive to succeed may not be. To qualify, someone in the story has to be doing something that specifically involves at least one of these criteria:

- an activity that is judged against a standard of excellence. ("He wrote the best essay in the class.")
- long-term involvement in reaching an achievement goal. ("She has been taking evening courses and studying to get her real-estate license.")
- an exceptional or unique accomplishment.

("He is trying to invent a new safety valve for hot air balloons.")

Other signs of achievement motivation to look for in a story include statements about wanting to succeed, looking forward to success, taking steps to achieve the goal, anticipating obstacles to success, and having either positive feelings about succeeding or negative feelings about failure.

Now turn to the next page and write a new story on the topic given. Don't spend more than four minutes on it. Your aim is to write a story that is *full of achievement themes*.

Once you've finished, read over this section again, then reread your story. Does it clearly fit one of the three criteria? How about the other signs we just looked at? How many of them are there?

Do you think you can do better? If so, give it a try with Story 2. Once again, when you're done, read it with a sharp eye for the presence or absence of achievement themes. Think about how you might have written a story with even more of them.

If you're serious about following this program, wait a week or two, reread this section, and write Story 3. Then wait two weeks before doing Story 4. Each time, once you've written the story, read it over carefully with the criteria in mind. Do you see an increase in the amount and kind of achievement concerns that show up in your stories?

Act Like a Motivated Person

I hope you saved your paper balls. If you didn't, make some more. You're going to play the paper toss game again.

I. Write a story about AN ARCHITECT AT A DRAFTING TABLE.

What is happening? Who are the people?

What led up to this situation? What happened in the past?

What is being thought and felt? What is wanted? By whom?

What will happen?

II. Write a story about TWO PEOPLE AT A MACHINE.

What is happening? Who are the people?

What led up to this situation? What happened in the past?

What is being thought and felt? What is wanted? By whom?

What will happen?

III. Write a story about A STUDENT WITH A NEW
COMPUTER.

What is happening? Who are the people?

What led up to this situation? What happened in
the past?

What is being thought and felt? What is wanted?
By whom?

What will happen?

IV. Write a story about A CHILD GAZING OUT THE WINDOW.

What is happening? Who are the people?

What led up to this situation? What happened in the past?

What is being thought and felt? What is wanted? By whom?

What will happen?

PAPER TOSS RECORD SHEET

THROW#	LINE#	HIT?(✓)
1		
2		
3		
4		
5		
6		
7		
8		
9		
10		
11		
12		
13		
14		
15		
16		
17		
18		
19		
20		

The first step is to get a clearer idea of your own personal skill level. Stand at what seems like an easy distance and take half a dozen tosses. If most of them went in, that line marks the near edge of your preferred range. If not, move one line closer and try again.

Now move back until you're at a distance that seems hard, and take another half dozen tosses. Did more than one go in? If not, that line marks the far edge of your preferred range. If so, move *back* one line and try again.

After you've found out what your preferred range is, make several score sheets like the one on the opposite page. Now you're ready to get down to some serious work.

Just as you did before, you are going to take twenty throws at the basket. But this time, you are going to remind yourself constantly to play *like someone with a strong motive to succeed*.

Here are some hints on how to do it. They aren't hard and fast rules, but you may find them helpful as a guide.

- For your first throw, stand somewhere toward the *far end* of your preferred range. In other words, make your job fairly challenging but not *too* hard.

- Any time you get two in a row into the basket from a particular line, move *back* one line for your next throw.

- Any time you miss two in a row from a particular line, move *forward* one line for your next throw.

One other hint: if you get so good at it that you're sinking most of your throws from the farthest line, give yourself a nice pat on the back. Then make the game harder. Use a smaller basket. Stand with your back to the basket and toss the balls over your shoulder. Do the whole thing with a bandanna tied over your eyes.

The purpose of this game is not to rack up points or to make you into a champion paper-ball tosser. It's

- to let you find out for yourself that it's more rewarding to choose tasks that are fairly challenging but doable.
- to start getting you into the *habit* of choosing that kind of task.

What matters, of course, is not the game itself. It's how you take the lessons you've learned in it and apply them to real life. Whenever the feeling of pride you'll get if you succeed is an important incentive, remember the paper toss. Ask yourself, "Have I chosen to take on a reasonable challenge? And if I opt for an even more challenging job, will I still have a fairly good chance of succeeding at it?"

Dealing With Anxiety About Failure

Important as it is, the motive to succeed is only half of achievement motivation. The other half, which plays just as important a role in influencing what we do, is our anxiety about failure.

Sometimes, as with Alan's ski weekend, this anxiety leads us to act in ways that ruin our chances of enjoying what we're doing. And sometimes, when it's more severe, it can leave us paralyzed, like a deer trapped in a car's headlights.

- After two grant proposals are rejected, a scientist closes down her research program rather than risk being rejected again.

- A student in a survey course fails the first exam. He knows the lowest mark will be eliminated, but he drops the course anyway.

- Someone who was recently laid off hears about a possible job opening but keeps putting off calling because he's afraid of what he'll hear. When he does finally call, the job has already been filled.

The good news is that there are ways of dealing with achievement anxiety. Here, briefly, are a couple of them.

Systematic relaxation. Get a stack of 3×5 index cards and write down short descriptions of situations that make you anxious. ("Telephoning a potential customer," "Waiting while an exam is being passed out," "Asking my boss for a raise," or what have you.) Write one situation on each card. Then do your best to arrange the cards according to *how much* anxiety each situation causes you.

Next, sit in a quiet place with the cards on your lap. As you read over the description on the top card, tighten all the muscles in your legs, then let go. Continue with your arms and hands, your stomach muscles, your shoulders and neck. Each time, wind up those muscles, then let every bit of tautness drain away. Imagine that your whole body is one big overcooked noodle.

After you've worked your way through all the major muscle groups, bring the next card to the top of the deck and do the same thing again. Do this for at least ten or fifteen minutes, preferably twice a day. Soon you'll be able to think about even the most anxiety-laden situation and stay relaxed. From this point, to staying relaxed when you are actually *in* the situation, is a shorter step than you might think.

Blowing it up. You've worked on relaxing while thinking about your annual performance appraisal, but now you have to walk into your supervisor's office for the actual appraisal. She's well known for asking people to compose their own appraisals, then making acid comments about them. You know that you're pretty good at your job, but so are some of the other people she's torn a strip off.

As you walk down the hall, your mouth is dry, your tongue feels three times its usual size, and your thoughts are skittering around in your head like cockroaches when you turn on the kitchen light. You realize that when you open your mouth, you'll be lucky to get out a "Duh!" if you don't just faint on the spot! You try to relax, but it doesn't seem to do any good. What now?

If relaxation won't relieve your anxiety, try giving in to it all the way and then some. You can think of this technique as visualization with a twist. Start imagining exactly how ghastly your meeting might be. Go the whole nine yards. Not only is your supervisor going to ridicule you, she's going to call in the whole department to watch her do it. In front of all your co-workers, she'll fire you and have the guards drag you out of the building by your ankles. Everyone will laugh at you.

Next, she'll make sure that you're turned down for

unemployment benefits. She'll get in touch with every other firm in the business and have you blacklisted. When the bank finds out, they'll call in your mortgage and cancel your credit cards. The local newspaper will print your photo on the front page, with the headline, "Loser of the Year." Your family will be so ashamed that they'll pretend they don't know you. By next month, you'll be out on the street, living in an old refrigerator carton.

At some point as you continue to visualize yourself, homeless and starving—and all because of the meeting you're about to have—a little good sense will kick in. However bad the next half hour may be, it can't *possibly* be as bad as you're imagining it. What if she *does* fire you? (And deep down, you know that the thought hasn't even crossed her mind.) Being out of work is no fun, but it's still miles better than living on the street. And as the gust of common sense blows away that cloud of exaggerated fear that you've allowed to gather around you, it will thin out your "normal" anxiety, too.

5

WHY DO WE SUCCEED OR FAIL?

How do we decide the reasons that something happened the way it did? We have a lot of different information we can use. There are the immediate circumstances, our past histories, the way we think human nature works, etc. But even people in the same situation will put that information together in different ways and reach different conclusions. One person might blame himself when something goes wrong, even if he's not remotely at fault. Another might find a way to blame others and see himself as an innocent victim.

These habits of thinking a certain way about why things happen show up especially clearly when people try to do something and either succeed or fail. For example, I've always liked cheese. As a kid, I was convinced that no one who knew what he was doing would think of eating apple pie without a slice of "rat trap" on top. In college, my friends and I decided that Liederkranz and sliced onions went perfectly with beer. (I hate to think what my breath must have been like!) And later, along with millions of other Americans, I learned that Brie is *supposed* to ooze all over the plate.

During a sabbatical year in France, I discovered that cheese isn't simply a food, it's an art form. When I shopped, I'd stop by the neighborhood cheesemonger (they still have such things in France), sample as many different varieties as the *fromagier* would allow, and take home some of the more interesting. When we traveled, I made a point of trying the specialties of the region. What I especially liked was going to a street market and buying a well aged goat cheese direct from the farmer who'd made it.

Then my doctor told me I had to get serious about my cholesterol level. I did, too. I eliminated eggs, went from half-and-half to 1% milk in my morning coffee, replaced butter with canola-oil spread, cut down on red meat . . . and stopped eating cheese. I didn't like it, but I did it.

One day, a friend had a small party. I arrived hungry, to discover that it was a wine-and-cheese-tasting party. Not only that, they were good cheeses, including one of my favorites, a *triple-crème* called St-André. I held out for a while, nibbling crackers and hovering on the other side of the room from the cheese table. But finally the temptation was too much. I ended up taking nibbles of four or five different cheeses and having two crackersworth of the St-André.

Afterwards, I couldn't stop berating myself. I had just blown my diet for good. I had proven that I had no willpower. In front of my friends, I had shown that I was, not just a glutton, but a *spineless* glutton. And because I was still hungry when I got home, I decided to fix myself a cheese omelet. Unable to stick to my diet, I no longer bothered trying.

Suppose that I'd put some of the responsibility on the circumstances—my arriving hungry, the lack of anything else to eat, and the general atmosphere of being with a bunch of people who are scarfing down crackers and cheese. That would have led me to a very different conclusion. I might have even decided that, all in all, I should be proud of myself for eating as little cheese as I did!

Instead when I fell off the cheese wagon, I was more prepared to think that the cause was my own weakness than to believe that the situation might have been responsible, because the way I habitually thought about success and failure led me toward that conclusion.

Most of us are in the habit of thinking a certain way about our successes and failures. And frequently, we're not even aware that it *is* a habit. If we think about it at all, we consider it simply the normal, ordinary way to look at the world. It doesn't occur to us that this habit may be actively getting in our way. And we can't even begin to change it until we know what it is.

Explaining Success and Failure

Take a close look at your own typical ways of thinking about success and failure. Give yourself ten or fifteen minutes to fill out the questionnaire that follows. For each item, put yourself in the situation that it describes. Imagine it as vividly as you can. Then decide which of the two alternatives is *most like* the reaction you would probably have, and circle it.

Remember, there are no right or wrong answers.

Even if you don't think either of the choices seems exactly like the way you would react, circle the one that comes closer. And do your best not to be swayed by how you think you *should* respond. Don't worry about what you think someone else might say about your choice. This is something you're doing for yourself, after all. To be really useful to you, your answers need to be as frank and open as possible.

For each item, circle *either* A or B. For now, disregard the symbols on the right.

1. You don't understand a colleague's
   proposal.   IT−
   A. I didn't listen carefully.   1
   B. My colleague didn't explain it
      well.   (0)

2. Your boss praises your recent work.   IL+
   A. I'm good at my job.   (1)
   B. He or she was in a good mood.   0

3. You're sure you grasp the details of
   an article you just read.   IL+
   A. The author explained his or her
      points well.   0
   B. I make a point of reading care-
      fully.   (1)

4. You tell a joke and nobody laughs.   IL−
   A. My friends have no sense of hu-
      mor.   0
   B. I've never been good at telling
      jokes.   (1)

5. You win a game of golf.   IT+
   A. I played well.   (1)
   B. The others played badly.   0

6. When you explain a new program to a co-worker, he or she doesn't understand.   IT—
   A. I didn't explain it well.   (1)
   B. My co-worker didn't listen carefully.   0

7. You overhear a colleague saying how bright you are.   IT+
   A. He or she wants something from me.   0
   B. I've had some great ideas lately.   (1)

8. You try a puzzle in a magazine and can't solve it.   IL—
   A. The instructions were badly written.   (0)
   B. I've never been very good at puzzles.   1

9. Your boss criticizes your work.   IT—
   A. I haven't been putting in enough efforts.   (1)
   B. He was in a rotten mood.   0

10. You clearly recall what the speaker said at a meeting.   IT+
    A. I made a point of concentrating on the speech.   1
    B. The speaker made his or her points well.   (0)

11. When you explain a complicated process to a friend, the friend understands.   IL+
    A. My friend is very bright.   0
    B. I'm good at explaining complicated subjects.   (1)

12. You lose a bridge game.   IL–
    A. My partner messed up.   0
    B. I'm not a very good player.   (1)

13. You get lost on the way to a friend's
    house.   IL–
    A. I've got a lousy sense of direction.   (1)
    B. My friend gave me lousy direc-
       tions.   0

14. You're chosen to receive an award
    from a community group.   IT+
    A. They were going down the list
       and got to my name.   0
    B. I've been especially active lately.   (1)

15. After you invest in a stock, the price
    falls dramatically.   IT–
    A. I happened to buy at just the
       wrong moment.   0
    B. I didn't investigate the company
       closely enough.   (1)

16. You tell a joke and everybody laughs.   IL+
    A. Everybody was in a good mood.   (0)
    B. I have a good sense of timing.   1

17. You fall while skiing.   IL–
    A. I'm not very athletic.   (1)
    B. The slope was icy.   0

18. You beat your usual tennis partner.   IT+
    A. I played unusually well.   (1)
    B. He played unusually badly.   0

19. After you invest in a stock, it soars.   IL+
    A. I always pick investments care-
       fully.   (1)
    B. I happened to get in at the right
       moment.   0

20. You can't follow the reasoning of
    an article.   IT—
    A. The article was confusing.   ⓪
    B. I didn't read it carefully.   1

Scoring Your Questionnaire

   For each of the four categories, count up your
total points. Write the totals in the blanks below.

IT+ _4_   IT— _3_   IL+ _4_   IL— _4_

As we go along, we'll explore how these scores tell
us about the ways we habitually explain our successes
and failures.

Are You An Innie Or An Outie?

   It was over thirty years ago that psychologist Julian
Rotter first turned a spotlight on an important difference in people's assumptions about how the world
works. When they face the possibility of doing something—whether it's applying for a promotion or complaining about a defective appliance—some people
generally expect that they will be able to have an effect on the outcome. Others expect just the opposite,
that outside forces will decide what happens. Rotter
called these two kinds of expectations *internal control*
and *external control*.
   Keep these two concepts in mind as you read the
following quotations. Can you tell which ones are
made by each type of person?

- "If I explain my reasoning, people will pay attention."
- "The cards are stacked against people like me."
- "What's the use of complaining? Nobody cares anyway."
- "Anyone who's willing to work hard can get ahead."
- "Students don't realize how much their grades are affected by how the teacher happens to be feeling that day."
- "People create their own luck."
- "Where there's a will, there's a way."
- "You can't fight City Hall."

A wise and impartial judge—if we could easily find such a person—would probably tell us that all of these statements are partly true and partly false. People will pay attention—sometimes. Hard work is rewarded—sometimes. And sometimes you can't fight City Hall—but other times you *can*.

Even so, you probably found yourself nodding in agreement to some of the statements, while thinking that others were more or less off the wall. Which ones did you think were more true to life? That should give you a clue to how you think about internal and external control.

Does it matter? Yes, of course it does. If you think you can affect what happens to you, you're more likely to try to do so. If you think that what you do doesn't make any difference, why bother? Here's an example: among people who are seriously ill, those who are more internal ask more questions about their disease than those who are more external. As a result, the internals know more about how they're doing and take a more active role in their own treatment.

This doesn't mean that always expecting to control your outcomes—being strongly internal—is automatically better for you. Let's face it, a lot of things that happen to us are beyond our control. I may be terrific at my job, but if the unit where I work is going to be phased out because of events thousands of miles away, there's not much point in telling myself, "Where there's a will, there's a way." Instead, maybe I should face the unpleasant fact that I *can't* control the disappearance of that job and focus my energies on areas of my life where I'm reasonably sure I really can have an impact.

Looking Forward and Looking Back

The concepts of internal control and external control have to do with whether we think we'll have an impact on what happens to us in the future. But it's at least as important to look at how we think about what has already happened to us. The question becomes, not what we expect, but where we think *responsibility* lies. Do we usually take the credit or blame for what happened to us? Or do we tend to assign credit or blame to outside forces?

- "I couldn't help it, the odds were against me."
- "I owe it all to hard work."
- "The exam was so easy that I aced it."
- "My friends led me astray."

- "I've never had a head for mathematics."
- "I couldn't have done it without the help of my partner."
- "I didn't work hard enough on the project."
- "I've always had a knack for that kind of problem."

We've all heard—and made—statements of this kind. They go all the way back to Adam, in the Garden of Eden: "The woman tempted me!" But recognizing them is just the first step. Next, we have to take a closer look at how they affect our motivation.

Before going any further, turn back to your scores on the questionnaire.

Add the scores for *IT+* and *IL+*.
Write the answer here: I+ = __8__
Add the scores for *IT−* and *IL−*.
Write the answer here: I− = __7__

As you've probably figured out, *I+* refers to giving internal reasons for success, and *I−* means giving internal reasons for failure. On each of these scales,

a score of 8, 9, or 10 means you are very internal
6 or 7 is fairly internal
5 is average
3 or 4 is fairly external
0, 1, or 2 is very external

The general rule is:

If you believe that your outcome (success or failure) was caused by *internal factors*, you will feel more strongly about it than if you believe it was caused by *external factors*.

In other words, being internal about your successes gives you a stronger feeling of pride than being external about them. And being internal about your failures makes you feel worse than being external about them.

Take Arnie and Sarah. They both received plaques as Employee of the Year in their division of a big corporation. Arnie told himself that he got the award because of his talent and hard work. Sarah believed that her supervisor had picked her because he thought it would look good to give the award to a woman this year. Which of them do you think has the plaque displayed prominently on his desk? Which one stuffed it away in a drawer?

It works in a similar way for failures. Let's say you've just finished hanging a picture. As you turn away, it crashes down, spraying shards of glass across the floor. What would make you feel worse? Telling yourself that the hook must have been defective (external)? Or that you'd done a lousy job of putting in the nail (internal)?

Either way, you'll still grumble about having to sweep up and replace the shattered glass. But in the one case, you'll *also* feel bad about having been personally responsible for the accident. In the other case, you won't.

This point applies to positive outcomes, too. Suppose you win a big lottery prize. You'll probably be very happy, even if you think that winning was a matter of pure luck (external). But if you're convinced that you won because of a secret system you invented (internal), then you're going to be very proud as well as happy, because you believe that you were *responsible* for winning.

Decision Rules and Attributions

How do we decide what caused a particular success or failure? To answer this question, we need to get acquainted with what's called *attribution theory*. This theory, developed largely by Bernard Weiner of UCLA, sets out to explain the factors that lead people to *attribute*, or assign, events to one cause or another.

We all use some of the same basic rules in making these decisions. See if you can figure out what rule you use in these examples:

- You take a course and get a D. You find out that practically everyone else in the course got a D or F. What do you think is more likely as the cause of your failure?

    It was a really tough course. (*external*) ✓

    —or—

    You're really bad at the subject. (*internal*)

- You take a course and get a D. You find out that practically everyone else in the course got an A or B. What do you think is more likely as the cause of your failure?

    It was a really tough course. (*external*)

    —or—

    You're really bad at the subject. (*internal*) ✓

- You go on a hike with a group of friends. At the end, you feel as if you could keep going for hours. Everyone else feels the same. What do you think is more likely as the cause of your success?

  It was a really easy hike. (*external*) ✓
  —or—
  You have unusual stamina. (*internal*)

- You go on a hike with a group of friends. At the end, you feel as if you could keep going for hours. Everyone else feels pooped. What do you think is more likely as the cause of your success?

  It was a really easy hike. (*external*)
  —or—
  You have unusual stamina. (*internal*) ✓

What did you say? Did you decide that the cause was external when your outcome was the same as it was for the others? Did you say it was internal when your outcome was different from theirs? If so, you were using one of the most common *decision rules* for making attributions.

There are others, too. For example, when we notice that we're gradually getting better at doing something, we tend to make an internal attribution for our success. We decide that we must be building up our strength, sharpening our skills, putting in the effort needed to improve. Conversely, if your performance steadily declines, you'll tend to blame that on internal causes, too, such as losing interest or getting bored.

Attributional Styles and Types

Knowing about the decision rules we use when we try to figure out why we succeeded or failed is a big step toward understanding ourselves and others. There's something we shouldn't overlook, however.

People don't always follow the rules.

As my daughter would say, "No, duh!" But as obvious as it may sound, this point helps us solve a major puzzle. How can people who have just gone through what seem like the same experiences end up with such different ideas about the causes?

Comments from average students who all got Cs on the same exam:

"I didn't study enough."

"The book is too confusing."

"I always mess up on multiple-choice questions."

"The questions were too tricky."

"I should have gone over my answers more carefully."

"I just don't have the head for this stuff."

and of course, that old favorite,

"You never told us we'd be responsible for that material."

Why such different reactions? The answer lies in our own individual *attributional styles*. When we think about why something happened to us, some of us lean toward an internal explanation and some toward an external explanation. The questionnaire that you completed a few pages ago is a way of getting an idea of how much you lean and in which direction.

Since the attributions we make for our failures and successes have a great deal to do with how we feel about them, these attributional styles have a big impact on our emotions. Once again, we feel more strongly about the successes and failures that we think were caused by internal factors.

That means that if we usually lean toward an internal explanation for our failures (high I−), we'll feel worse about them than someone who leans the other way (low I−). And it's similar with success. If you favor an internal explanation for your successes (high I+), you'll feel better about them than someone who leans toward an external explanation (low I+).

Both these tendencies, I+ and I−, are important, but it's the way a particular individual combines them that's crucial. The reason for this is simple. Whether we're looking at careers, or sports, or even hobbies, practically all of us have uneven records. Sometimes we succeed, sometimes we don't.

That's true even of champions. World class athletes have bad days and even bad seasons. Nobel Prize-winning novelists write occasional duds. Picasso sometimes painted pictures that made him wrinkle his nose in distaste. How they—or we—explain those failures is just as important as how they explain success.

When we look at these two elements, attributions for success and failure, together, we find that we're describing four distinct types of people:

• HIGH I+, HIGH I−	Reacts strongly to both successes and failures.
• HIGH I+, LOW I−	Proud of successes, not disturbed by failures.
• LOW I+, HIGH I−	Ashamed of failures, not proud of successes.
• LOW I+, LOW I−	Doesn't react much to successes *or* failures.

Keep in mind that most of us don't lean all that much in either the internal or the external direction. There aren't that many people who will seriously believe that winning the lottery is mainly a matter of personal skill, or who decide that a consistent string of successes is really the result of pure luck. We'll find it useful to think of people—ourselves, to begin with—as basically fitting into one of these four types, but in most cases we won't be talking about *extreme* examples of a particular type.

Deciding What to Expect Next

During their training to become customers' reps with a major brokerage house, Greg and Dino filled out a questionnaire similar to the one at the beginning of this chapter. Their scores showed both of them to be moderately internal for both success and failure. After six months on the job, the two were perform-

ing at about the same level. They both had their share
of success and failure. As their questionnaire scores
would predict, they were both proud of their successes
and unhappy over their failures.

At the end of the probation period, Dino was enthusiastic about his position. He was sure that he had
a great future in the securities business. Greg, on the
other hand, was so discouraged that he was actively
planning to quit and go into a different field. What
happened?

Listen to them talk about how they explain their
positive and negative experiences.

   Dino: "Whenever things went well, it was like
   a sign. Hey, I've got what it takes to get ahead!
   Sure, I had some setbacks. Who doesn't? I must
   not have put in enough effort. The only answer
   to that is, try harder next time."

   Greg: "By really busting my butt, I usually
   managed to hold up my end. But if I ever
   slacked off even a little, I'd get shot down. I
   know why, too. I just don't have the right head
   for this business."

Before you go on to the next paragraph, ask yourself this: What causes are Dino and Greg using to
explain their successes and failures? Do they use the
same ones? Or different?

Let's look first at success. Dino sees his successes
as stemming from something about himself, an internal quality that is stable or long-lasting ("I've got
what it takes."). Greg also sees his successes as the
result of something about himself, something internal,

but in his case, that something is an unusual effort ("busting my butt").

There's a big difference in their explanations for failure, too. In both cases, they think the causes lie within themselves. But Dino believes that his failures stemmed from not trying hard enough ("I must not have put in enough effort"). Greg saw his failures as proof that he lacked the ability to succeed ("I just don't have the right head").

Causes, Lasting and Temporary

Bernard Weiner, who's already been mentioned as one of the big names in attribution theory, points out how important it is to pay attention to the difference between causes that are *stable* or *lasting* (ability, talent, an easy task, etc.) and those that are *unstable* or *temporary* (an unusual effort, good or bad luck, etc.). These explanations offer clues to what's likely to happen in the future.

Once again, there is a general rule:

If you believe that an outcome (a success or failure) was the result of a *stable, lasting* cause, you'll expect a similar outcome the next time you're in a similar situation.

If you believe that the outcome was the result of an *unstable, temporary* cause, you won't necessarily expect a similar outcome the next time you're in a similar situation.

To see how this works out in real life, let's take a closer look at Dino and Greg.

When Dino succeeds, he usually believes that the

reason was a lasting cause—his ability. If you ask him how he expects to do next time, what will he answer? Unless he's trying to look modest, he'll say, "Well, I've already shown I have the ability I need to succeed, and it's not going to vanish, is it? So I'd say I have a very good shot at succeeding next time, too."

When Dino fails, he sees it as the result of a temporary cause—not enough effort. So if you ask him how he expects to do next time, he'll tell you, "I know I just failed, but that was because I didn't try hard enough. Since I mean to try a lot harder next time, I expect to do a lot better."

Greg's way of understanding his successes and failures has very different results. When he succeeds, he tends to think of it as coming from an unusual effort—"busting my butt." Ask how he expects to do next time, and he's likely to say, "I don't know . . . if I can get it together to make the same kind of effort, I might pull it off. But if I don't, I won't. I'll blow it for sure."

Failure he sees as the natural result of a basic lack of ability. What does he expect next time? "What's going to change? I can't go down to the mall and buy myself some more ability. If I failed this time, why shouldn't I expect to fail next time, too?"

Over the long run, these differences lead to an astonishing result. Dino will approach new situations with the expectation that he will succeed, and Greg will approach them with the expectation that he will fail—*even when they have both had the same degree of success and failure in the past!*

Are You More Like Dino or Like Greg?

You probably found yourself thinking that either Greg or Dino sounded more like you than the other did. You also probably saw bits of yourself in both Greg *and* Dino. That's not surprising. Most of us think a little like one and a little like the other, but lean more in one direction.

Here's a way of getting a clearer idea about which direction and how much. First, for convenience, copy the scores from page 102 here:

IT+ _4_ IT– _3_ IL+ _4_ IL– _4_

(handwritten annotations above boxes: Good Success · Temp Fail · Lasting Success · Lasting Fail)

We already know that + stands for Success and – stands for Failure, and it's not too hard to work out that T means *Temporary* and L means *Lasting*. So IT+, for example, means a tendency to give *I*nternal, *T*emporary explanations for success. For each of these four scales,

    a score of 5 is very high
    4 is fairly high
    2 or 3 is average
    1 is fairly low
    0 is very low

Which of the scales do you think Dino would have high and low scores on? If your answer is that he would be high on IT– and IL+, and low on IT+ and IL–, then you've clearly grasped what the scales are about. Greg, by contrast, would have high IT+ and IL− scores, and low IT− and IL+ scores.

Notice that we need to take the scores on *all* the scales into account. If we're looking at a success, it's not just attributing it to lasting causes that helps raise expectations, but at the same time *not* attributing it to temporary causes. We can put this in the form of a number:

Take your score for IL+:	4
Add 5 points to it:*	+ 5
subtotal:	9
Now *subtract* your IT+ score:	− 4
ILT+:	5

The larger this number is, the more likely it is that your general expectations will tend to go *up* after a *success*.

We can summarize reactions to failure in the same way:

*The reason for adding the points is to avoid any negative numbers that might be confusing.

Take your score for IL−:   4

Add 5 points to it: +   5
        subtotal: 9

Subtract your IT− score: − 4 3

        ILT−:   6

The larger *this* number is, the more likely it is that your general expectations will tend to go *down* after a *failure*.

For both ILT+ and ILT−,

    a score of 9 or 10 is very high

    7 or 8 is fairly high

    4, 5, or 6 is average

    2 or 3 is fairly low

    0 or 1 is very low

Before we leave Greg and Dino, here's a simple table that will give you a more precise answer to the question we started the section with: are you more like Dino or like Greg?

	ILT+	ILT−
DINO	HIGH	LOW
GREG	LOW	HIGH
YOU	AVG	AVG

The Specific and the General

Nicole and Melissa got to know each other at business school and started meeting regularly for lunch to talk about their lives and careers. When Nicole missed out on an important promotion, she was crushed. She told Melissa the next time she saw her, "I know perfectly well why it happened. That old so-and-so who heads up my division goes into a cold sweat at the thought of having to work with a woman who's anything more than a glorified clerk."

"What are you going to do?" asked Melissa.

Nicole shrugged. "Go on with my life," she replied. "Angle for a transfer to another division. And, just in case, start polishing my resumé."

A few months later, Melissa had a similar setback at work. She fell apart. She quit repainting her apartment halfway through, stopped going to the health club, and abandoned her diet. "What's the point?" she told Nicole, staring down at her plate. "I might as well face it, it doesn't matter what I do. I've just hit the famous glass ceiling. The cards are stacked against someone like me."

*   *   *

Can we use what we've learned about attributional styles to help us understand Nicole and Melissa? At first, it doesn't seem so. Both of them see their failure as being the result of a cause that is *external* and *lasting* (the boss's prejudice; the "glass ceiling"). Yet their reactions to not being promoted were very different.

The reason is that there's another important feature of people's attributional styles that we haven't talked about yet, one that doesn't show up in your questionnaire scores. Take a close look at the following pairs of statements:

I lost the tennis match because I'm not good at playing tennis.	I lost the tennis match because I'm not good at sports.
I missed getting the new account because I didn't work hard enough at it.	I missed getting the new account because I don't work hard enough.
I got a low grade in the course because the teacher has a prejudice against me.	I got a low grade in the course because teachers have a prejudice against me.
The research project was a failure because my hypothesis was wrong.	The research project was a failure because my approach is wrong.
The evening with my new date went badly because she doesn't find me attractive.	The evening with my new date went badly because women don't find me attractive.
The gourmet French meal I fixed for friends was a disaster because I'm not good at cooking that kind of food.	The gourmet French meal I fixed for friends was a disaster because I'm not good at cooking.

The reasons in each pair are similar in terms of internal vs. external and lasting vs. temporary. But those on the left are *specific* to the particular situation, while those on the right are much more *general*. It's the difference between thinking, "I did badly because I'm not good at this kind of thing," and "I did badly because I'm stupid."

Both these attributions are painful and discouraging. But when the reasons we give ourselves for an outcome are more general, *too* general, so are the implications we draw from that outcome. The expectations that we form get stretched to cover situations far removed from the one that led to the outcome. It's a process my father liked to call, "Drawing vast conclusions from half-vast data."

In an earlier chapter, I told about an experience I had in elementary school art class. The attribution I made was that I had failed because I was utterly without artistic talent. Internal, lasting—and very general.

It didn't have to be that way. I *could* have come to the conclusion that I had no talent for watercolors, or for drawing trees, or for drawing trees the particular way Mrs. Norman thought people ought to draw trees. Any of those attributions would have been just as internal, just as lasting. They probably would have made me feel just as rotten and discouraged at the time. But they would not have led me to shy away from the visual arts for years afterwards.

Notice that we've been looking only at examples of overgeneralized attributions for negative outcomes—failures. That isn't an accident or oversight. Anytime we see a failure as the result of a very general cause, it has negative consequences.

The case of success is more complicated. Suppose you try a computer game, do well, and decide, "I must be really good at computer games.'' Will that lead to overconfidence? Maybe, but that isn't so bad. You'll probably decide to try other computer games, expecting to do well. If you do, fine. And if you don't, if your attribution really was too general, you'll find it out quickly enough.

On the other hand, if overconfidence may have seriously negative results, overgeneralizing from success may be just as dangerous as overgeneralizing from failure. Not long ago, my daughter informed me that she knows how to drive. When I looked surprised, she said, ''Well, I was awesome on the bumper cars at the fair the other day. It's the same thing, right? You push down on the pedal and turn the wheel.''

I like the fact that she sees herself as competent, but it gives me a chill to imagine her deciding to try out her supposed skill behind the wheel of a real car.

Are Some Attributional Habits Better Than Others?

We saw a couple of chapters back how powerfully our expectations can affect our achievements. Now we see how powerfully the explanations we give ourselves—our attributions—can affect our expectations, as well as affecting the feelings of pride and shame that we have about our successes and failures.

The implication is obvious:

Developing a positive attributional style is a key element in motivating ourselves, both to succeed and to get past failure.

What we do always matters, but if we're looking at
the long term consequences of what we do, then how
we *think about* what we do matters even more.

Let's face it, any of us may find himself or herself
up against an unexpected obstacle. Your firm's major
client goes Chapter 11. The morning of a big pres-
entation, there's a wildcat train strike and you're three
hours late. Just after you accept an important position
with a federal agency, Congress decides that the na-
tion can get along without your agency.

How do you react? Do you fall apart, like Melissa?
Do you brood for a while, then get back to your usual
activities, but resolve not to be lured into having high
hopes again? Do you acknowledge the setback without letting it throw you? The answer is going to depend very much on how you explain the setback to
yourself. And the way we explain our successes is just
as important.

What *is* the best pattern of explanations? Researchers have found that people with high achievement motivation are more likely to:

- attribute their successes to both *ability* (IL+)
  and high *effort* (IT+);

- attribute their failures to insufficient *effort*
  (IT−).

This is a lot like the pattern we saw in Dino. People
with this attributional style will feel good after a success and bad after a failure. Their expectations of future success will go up after a success, but won't
necessarily go down—and might even go up—after a
failure.

I can hear some of you mutter, "How's that again?"

What's so great about feeling bad after a failure? And why should I expect to do *better* after failing?"

The answers to both those questions have to do with some peculiar features of effort attributions. We put an especially high value on successes that seem to happen through trying hard, whether they're our own successes or someone else's. Think of the story about Abe Lincoln as a boy, studying his schoolbooks by firelight. He would have learned at least as well, probably better, if his parents could have afforded an oil lamp. But then his success wouldn't have been quite such a triumph.

In the same way, we're toughest on ourselves (and on others) when we think a failure came from *not* trying hard. Suppose you ask a friend for help. If he can't help you, that's too bad, but you won't hold it against him. But if he doesn't *try* to help, your opinion of him is likely to change abruptly.

We think of trying or not trying as a matter of personal responsibility. I can't choose to be talented or untalented at something, but I *can* choose whether or not to work hard at it. If I choose to work hard, and I succeed, that success is more deeply mine than if it had come easily. And if I don't work hard at it, and fail, it means that I *chose* to fail. As the saying goes, I've no one to blame but myself.

However, painful as it is to blame a failure on lack of effort, that blame has a very important positive side, too. I'm telling myself, "I failed because I didn't try hard enough." But that's basically the same as saying, "*If* I try harder, I can succeed." That raises my expectations for the future, at the same time that it motivates me to try harder. And if the activity I'm involved in is sensitive to increased effort—as so much of what we do is—I'll discover that I've increased, not just my expectations, but my real chances of success as well.

Changing Your Attributional Style

By staying with me this far, you've already made a start at changing the way you habitually think about success and failure in a more positive direction. That's because the first step in changing those habits is *recognizing* and *examining* them.

What you've done already—filling out the questionnaire at the beginning of the chapter, then reading about what different answers mean—is like sitting down with a field guide to birds to study the pictures and read the descriptions. There's some information that seems very familiar, some that may or may not apply, and some that sounds pretty remote. But the only way you'll be sure which sort is which is by taking your guide out into the field and using it to identify live birds.

That's something like what you're about to do now. The questionnaire asked you to imagine yourself in a series of situations and think how you would react. Now, over the next three days, take notes on about half a dozen *real* situations and look closely at how you actually *do* react. For each entry, there are three sections:

- an ACTIVITY

- an ATTRIBUTION and

- an AFTERMATH

Here's an example:

ACTIVITY

I tried to . . . *set up a lunch date with someone I met recently.*
The outcome was . . . *he said he couldn't, that he's snowed under with work for the next few weeks.*

ATTRIBUTION

This happened because . . . *people I try to be friendly with just don't want to bother with me.*

AFTERMATH

I feel . . . *disappointed, hurt, and angry; like someone who can simply be brushed aside.*
In a similar situation, I expect . . . *to be rejected again.*

The activities you look at don't have to be earthshaking. Our attributional styles affect how we react to losing a quarter in a pay phone just as much as to winning an important court case. Anything you do that leads to a positive or negative outcome can help give you new insights into your own attributional style.

The one thing that's essential is that you be candid. If you feel unsure about writing such personal accounts in the pages of a book, make a photocopy of the next few pages and keep it with your private notebook.

ACTIVITY

I tried to . . .

The outcome was . . .

ATTRIBUTION
  This happened because . . .

AFTERMATH
  I feel . . .

  In a similar situation, I expect . . .

ACTIVITY
  I tried to . . .

  The outcome was . . .

ATTRIBUTION
  This happened because . . .

AFTERMATH
  I feel . . .

  In a similar situation, I expect . . .

ACTIVITY
  I tried to . . .

  The outcome was . . .

ATTRIBUTION
  This happened because . . .

AFTERMATH
  I feel . . .

  In a similar situation, I expect . . .

ACTIVITY
I tried to . . .

The outcome was . . .

ATTRIBUTION
This happened because . . .

AFTERMATH
I feel . . .

In a similar situation, I expect . . .

ACTIVITY
I tried to . . .

The outcome was . . .

ATTRIBUTION
This happened because . . .

AFTERMATH
I feel . . .

In a similar situation, I expect . . .

ACTIVITY
I tried to . . .

The outcome was . . .

ATTRIBUTION
  This happened because . . .

AFTERMATH
  I feel . . .

  In a similar situation, I expect . . .

As you look over what you've written, pay attention, first, to the kinds of attributions you made for different kinds of activities and outcomes. For instance, do you use more lasting and general causes to explain failures than to explain successes? Is there a different pattern for social activities (discussing something with a friend, making a suggestion to the boss, etc.) than for solitary activities (playing a computer game, fixing a broken doorbell, etc.)?

Second, notice how the attributions you made have a direct connection to the emotions you felt and the expectations you developed afterwards. It's a matter of cause and effect. If something I undertake turns out well (or badly), how I feel and what I expect next come mainly, not from the outcome itself, but from my beliefs about what caused that outcome. And *beliefs can be changed.* In place of beliefs that harm us and hold us back, we can actively work to encourage beliefs that will help us.

Of course we shouldn't try to ignore reality, but "reality" is much more complicated than our ideas about it. Even the simplest event has many different levels of causes. For example, if you get angry after another driver cuts you off, you could see that as the result of biochemistry, evolutionary history, brain physiology, your childhood, your adult personality, your general mood in recent weeks, and the argument you had with a co-worker earlier in the day. You could, but who has the time and energy? So instead, you pick what seems like the most obvious or relevant cause. You may say to yourself, "I've got such a terrible temper," and leave it at that.

The problem is, so many of us tend to pick causes that minimize our successes and make setbacks seem like catastrophes. The other day, I was talking to a graduate student who had just completed her course work for the doctorate with a nearly perfect straight-A record. When I congratulated her, she shook her head and said, "I know, I really lucked out, but I'm sure it's going to catch up with me."

Luck? Give me a break! A dozen different professors, over a four or five year period, all thought her work was excellent. So why doesn't she take their word for it? And the worst part is, when she does suffer a setback—as all of us do now and then—she's likely to believe that "it" has finally caught up with her and conclude that she's reached the beginning of the end.

Imagine how much happier and more productive she would be if she looked at that grade record and said to herself, "So far, my talent and hard work have paid off. There's no reason why that shouldn't continue. If I run into an obstacle, I'll do what I can to deal with it, and based on what's happened up to now, I think I've got a good chance of succeeding." The facts support that interpretation at least as well as they do the way she now looks at her situation. But how does she get from here to there?

Active Argument

One of the very best ways to overcome a bad habit is to replace it with a better one. If you're in the habit of making pessimistic, self-defeating attributions for your outcomes—and by now, you certainly know if that's a description of you—your goal should be to get into the habit of making optimistic, self-enhancing attributions instead. You've already taken the first step of recognizing and examining the beliefs that are holding you back. The next stage is to *combat* them by using *active argument*.

You've already met this technique before, in the chapter on expectations. To refresh your memory, here's how it works. When you realize that you've just made a lasting and general attribution for a failure, or a temporary one for a success, start looking for alternate explanations and evidence, and *argue* with yourself. Imagine that you're in a conversation with someone you don't particularly like or trust (one of those conversations where the other person starts off with, "Well, for your own good, I'll be *perfectly* frank . . .") and you find that attribution of yours being hurled at you as an accusation. Are you going to sit still for that? Of course not!

Here's how it might work with the example we looked at a few pages back. You try to make a lunch date with someone you met recently, he says he's too busy, and you decide that the reason is that people simply don't want to get friendly with you (lasting, general). What would you say if someone else tried to tell you that about yourself?

"Hey, hold on! Maybe I'm not going to win the Most Popular title, but I've got friends, and some of them I'm very close to. Anyway, this guy was very friendly when I met him. As a matter of fact, he was the one who suggested we get together. I just happened to be the one who called first. And I remember, he said what a busy period this was going to be for him. And even if it doesn't work out with him, for whatever reason, that doesn't say anything about how other people might feel about me."

Now it's your turn. Over the next few days, pay attention, take notes, and *argue*.

ACTIVITY
I tried to . . .

The outcome was . . .

ATTRIBUTION
This happened because . . .

AFTERMATH
I feel . . .

In a similar situation, I expect . . .

ARGUMENT
My initial attribution was wrong because . . .

ACTIVITY
I tried to . . .

The outcome was . . .

ATTRIBUTION
This happened because . . .

AFTERMATH
I feel . . .

In a similar situation, I expect . . .

ARGUMENT
My initial attribution was wrong because . . .

ACTIVITY
I tried to . . .

The outcome was . . .

ATTRIBUTION
This happened because . . .

AFTERMATH
I feel . . .

In a similar situation, I expect . . .

ARGUMENT
My initial attribution was wrong because . . .

ACTIVITY
I tried to . . .

The outcome was . . .

ATTRIBUTION
This happened because . . .

AFTERMATH
I feel . . .

In a similar situation, I expect . . .

ARGUMENT
My initial attribution was wrong because . . .

If this feels artificial at first, don't give up. The goal is to recognize negative, self-defeating attributions and argue against them, *before* they've had time to affect your feelings and expectations. With practice, you'll reach it, and you may find it's a lot easier than you think. More than that, as your arguments get more convincing, you'll come to realize that you've developed a new attributional style that has made you happier and more hopeful.

6

STAYING IN FOR THE LONG HAUL

Have you ever had the feeling that you are being slowly eaten alive by an endless series of dull, repetitive chores? You need to buy groceries, to finish that report your boss wants, to pick up the cleaning, to speak to your kid's teacher about his reading scores, to weed the garden, to rotate the tires on the car, to make a dentist appointment, and isn't it way past time to defrost the fridge?

The worst part is, you already know that tomorrow will bring another batch to add to the list of tasks that you didn't quite manage to get to today.

Listen to these voices for echoes of yourself.

- "I spend so much of my life doing things that don't really matter to me."
- "I'm constantly pushing myself."
- "Everybody wants a piece of me, and I don't seem to be able to turn them down."
- "I keep going round and round and never get anywhere."
- "By the time I get done with the things I have

to do, I'm too worn out even to think about doing something I *want* to do."

Usually, the things we "have to do" can be sorted into two boxes, one marked *Routine* and another marked *Urgent*. Both types have a peculiar advantage—they rescue us from having to decide what to do. Routine tasks we do because we always do them. Urgent tasks we do because we don't think we have any choice. It's worth noticing, though, that in both cases, there's one question that generally doesn't come up. Does accomplishing this task really *matter*? And if so, in what way and to whom?

What if it's something that matters to someone else, but not to you? Does that mean you refuse to do it? Not necessarily. All of us have taken on various roles—spouse, parent, employee, citizen—that bring with them certain obligations as well as privileges. The scales come with the fish.

Let's say my wife wants to invite certain friends of hers to dinner. I may not particularly want to spend an evening with those people. I certainly don't want to wash up after them. Even so, I'll do it—graciously, I hope. After all, I knew when I got married that part of the deal involved giving up some of my freedom to choose how to spend my time.

If my department chair assigns me to teach a particular course next semester and I don't want to, I can certainly explain my objections and hope for a change in my schedule. But when push comes to shove, unless there is a change, I'll teach that course. That's my job. If I want to go on holding it, I'm obligated to do what it requires.

Even then, however, I'm making a choice. What if I were ordered to teach something that I thought was unprofessional, or even immoral? I could appeal to the dean, the president, the trustees. I could try to interest the press and sympathetic public figures in my case. If all else failed, I could quit. The consequences would be painful, but the choice would still be mine.

Constraints and Choices

Obviously, I am not trying to convince you that you can freely choose to be or do anything you like. Our age, sex, race, education, economic status, physical condition, and personal history all place practical limits on us. It's only sensible to make a realistic survey of what these limits are and accept them, instead of wasting time on "If only . . ." daydreams.

As a male, I can't choose to become pregnant (at least not with our present technology). I can't decide that I would rather have been born into a different family, region, or century. I can't decide to take off a few months from work, not if I want to keep food on the table and a roof over my family's heads. And speaking of heads, I can't even choose to have kept more of my hair, or to hold onto what's left of it.

Too often, however, we overlook areas where we *do* have choice. We assume that even there, we are controlled by outside factors—other people, the economy, "destiny." The result is that we don't do a good job of deciding when we actually have the power to do so. Then we complain to ourselves about feeling bossed around.

When we do make choices, do we find ways to make them that will serve our own best interests? Or do we fall back on ways that relieve us of the burden

of choosing? Is it freedom of choice that we want, or
is it really freedom *from* choice?

Let's say that you have a family vacation coming
up. There are lots of possibilities for how to spend it.

- *Follow the pack*—You know three different
  people at work who are planning to visit
  Grand Cayman Island this year. It doesn't
  sound that different from a dozen other island
  destinations, but your colleagues must know
  something you don't.

- *Daydream*—Every time you pick up a travel
  magazine, you start imagining a trip to still
  another exotic destination that you know you
  can't afford. Whatever you end up doing on
  your vacation, it's bound to be a letdown by
  comparison with your dreams.

- *Do what you've always done*—For years, your
  family's been going to the same area in the
  mountains or at the shore. It's not very relaxing or stimulating, but at least it's familiar.

- *Act on impulse*—You see an attractive poster
  in the window of a travel agency and book a
  tour on the spot.

- *Decide by default*—You put off making a decision, then end up at the only place where you
  can still get a reservation.

If none of this matters that much, if to you a vacation is just a vacation, then suppose that your boss
has asked you to recommend a future direction for the
firm. You are faced with some of the same possibilities. You could suggest doing the same thing that
your competitors are doing, or advise doing what

you've been doing all along, or go with the first hot idea that strikes you. Or you could put off the problem until the last minute, then hand in a report that's held together with chewing gum and baling wire.

There isn't necessarily anything wrong with following a long tradition, or listening to the recommendations of others, or dreaming about an experience that you're not likely to have any other way, as long as you're sure that you're satisfied with the decisions that you reach by those means. But if you're *not* happy with the results you're getting, or if you realize that you use those means because it's easier than trying to break out of your rut, then it's time to take a new approach, one that's based on thinking about what you really want and how to get it.

"That sounds great in theory," you might protest. "But it takes every bit of energy I've got just to keep my head above water. What am I supposed to do, let myself drown?"

If the only alternative is drowning, by all means keep treading water! Raise your head from time to time, however, and look around. There may be land in sight. And if there is, every stroke you've been making just to stay afloat could be carrying you toward it.

Seeing and Defining Your Goals

How can we give meaning and a sense of direction to our daily activities? In terrible times—war, economic disaster, serious illness—simply surviving to another day may be a triumphant achievement. But even then, people are better off if they have a clear idea of their goals.

The exercise at the beginning of Chapter Four gave you a close look at one of your important specific goals. Now let's try to get a more global idea of what you think might be worth working toward.

Take your notebook and a pen or pencil. Go somewhere quiet and write out an answer to this question:

How do I want to be living my life two years from now?

Let your mind go. Don't worry about being practical or realistic. Put down your thoughts as quickly as they come to you, without censorship. You're not committing yourself to any of the ideas you list. No one is going to put what you write in the newspaper for your friends and enemies to read. You don't even have to show it to anyone, however close, unless you decide that you want to.

While you're making up your mind about giving this a try, here's *my* try:

Two years from now, I'd like to be sitting in the garden of an old farmhouse in Provence, working on a sequel to this book. The sun is shining, the birds are chirping, and the breeze from the hillside carries the scent of wild thyme. My wife is upstairs, writing an article about the recent theatre festival in a nearby town, and my daughter has set up her easel under a tree to try her hand at painting a landscape.

From the open kitchen window comes the aroma of lunch—chicken with tomatoes, garlic, onions, olives, and fresh rosemary. When I come to a place in my writing that gives me trouble, I go inside and give the pot a stir. When I come to a *really* difficult place, I work up a sweat restoring an old stone wall. After lunch, we take a drive to the village in a little blue convertible. The top is down, and there's a tape of vintage French accordion music playing.

Of course, this is a fantasy. I may want to have a farmhouse in Provence and a blue convertible, but I don't have them now and I don't have any solid reason to think that I ever will. More important, my daughter would probably put roach powder in my Pernod if I dared to drag her across the Atlantic, so far away from all her friends in the USA.

The point, however, is that *fantasies have power*. They energize us, and they give direction to that energy. They do what engineers call "pushing the envelope," enlarging the scope of what we think of as possible and keeping us from foreclosing on our potential. Wishing alone won't let you realize the fantasies, but it is an essential first step.

Ordering Your Priorities

As you look over what you've written, you'll notice that a number of different elements or themes show up. All these details have some degree of importance to you, or you wouldn't have included them. At the same time, we know that they aren't all equally important. When it comes to setting priorities, how do we find out which goal elements are *most* important?

We're going to make use of a well known technique of psychological measurement called the *paired comparisons method*. Here's how to do it.

First, go through what you wrote with a pencil or Hi-Lighter and select the four elements that you think have the greatest significance to you. List them here. Don't worry about trying to put them in any particular order.

		Element	Score
#1	1.	_Business_	_4_
#2	2.	_Financially secure_	_1_
#4	3.	_Social life_	_1_
#3	4.	_Good shape_	_2_

Next, write each of the numbered elements, or a convenient abbreviation for it, next to its number in the blanks below. Notice that each element shows up in three different places.

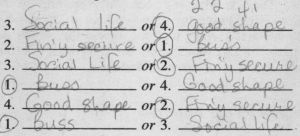

3. _Social life_ or (4.) _Good shape_
2. _Fin'y secure_ or (1.) _Bus's_
3. _Social Life_ or (2.) _Fin'y secure_
(1.) _Buss_ or 4. _Good shape_
4. _Good shape_ or (2.) _Fin'y secure_
(1.) _Buss_ or 3. _Social life_

Now look at each pair of elements and compare them. Ask yourself which of the two is *more important*. On the first line, for example, you'll compare #3 with #4. Let's say that #3 is "Keeping fit" and #4 is "Have my own business." Which of those two is more important *to you*? Once you decide, circle or check it. Then go on to the next pair. Keep doing this until you've circled one of the two in each pair.

Finally, count the number of times that each goal element is checked or circled. That is its score. The goal element with the biggest score is the one you think is most important, the one with the second biggest score is the next most important, and so on.

This order of priorities isn't carved in stone, by the way. It's more like a snapshot of how you think at this moment. If, a few weeks or months from now, you write another story about how you'd like to be living your life in two years, it's not likely to sound exactly the same. Some different goal elements will show up, and the order of those that are the same will be a little different, too. Life moves on, and we change with it.

My Own Priorities

Here's an illustration of how to use the paired comparisons technique. As I read through the story I wrote, these are the elements that strike me as most significant:

1. <u>Living in France—Provence</u>
2. <u>Writing as a career—next book</u>
3. <u>Outdoors—garden, sunlight, breezes</u>
4. <u>Family life—wife and child</u>

I'm afraid that the delicious chicken dish and the sporty little blue convertible didn't make the cut.

Now for the comparisons themselves:

3. <u>Outdoors</u>	*or* √4.	<u>Family</u>
2. <u>Writing</u>	*or* √1.	<u>France</u>
3. <u>Outdoors</u>	*or* √2.	<u>Writing</u>
1. <u>France</u>	*or* √4.	<u>Family</u>
√4. <u>Family</u>	*or* 2.	<u>Writing</u>
√1. <u>France</u>	*or* 3.	<u>Outdoors</u>

Some of the choices are easy. Would I rather spend time outdoors, or with my family? For me, family easily wins the day. But what about the next pair, Writing or France? Suppose I had the means to live in France, but my agent solemnly told me that such a move would be the end of my career as a writer? What then? I'm sitting here, chewing on a knuckle, trying to figure out how I really want to answer the question.

Finally, I'll put a check mark next to France, as more important to me *at this time*. After all, if I were living there, I could still go on writing, even if nobody wanted to publish or read what I wrote.

After going through each of the other pairs in the same way, I end up with these scores:

Family	3
France	2
Writing	1
Outdoors	0

I can't claim that I'm very surprised by the way this came out. I could have easily predicted that Family would take the top spot. I'm not sure that I would have gotten the order of the other goal elements exactly right, but I wouldn't have been too far off. Even so, this exercise is valuable as a way to help us shine a bright light on our goals and priorities.

Here's an example. In a couple of hours, my daughter is coming home after four weeks at summer camp. This is the first time she's been away from home for so long. This morning, when I planned my day, I blocked in enough time to pick her up, to help unpack her footlocker, and to spend a little while chatting with her.

After completing the paired comparisons, however, I've decided to rethink my priorities and devote more than "a little while" to being with her. I can catch up on the writing later tonight, after she's asleep.

Working Toward Long Range Goals: Why Is It So Hard?

If you did the exercises so far in this chapter, you now have a clearer picture of your long-term goals and priorities. That was one of the things you really wanted and felt you needed. So why don't you feel more elated? Why do you have that sudden impulse to put down the book and make up a shopping list, do a wash, leaf through a recent catalogue, or turn on the television?

We all know the reason, whether we let ourselves acknowledge it or not:

Trying to accomplish a long range goal usually feels difficult and unrewarding.

If you keep a weekly to-do list, go through it for the last few weeks and sort the items out into Short-Term and Long-Term. Now go through it again and sort them into Done and Not Done. Enter the results in the table on the next page:

	DONE	NOT DONE
SHORT TERM		
LONG TERM		

What most people find when they look over the result is that *short-term tasks get done* and *long-term tasks don't*.

I should point out that, by getting you to compile a table of this sort, I've stacked the deck in favor of my argument. One reason short-term tasks get done more often is *because* they're short-term.

Let's say that one of your short-term tasks is flossing your teeth, and one of your long-term tasks is getting your college degree. If you're conscientious about it, you'll be able to check off flossing as done seven or even fourteen times a week. You won't get to check off graduating from college more than once in four years or so. But that's not just a trick of logic. As we'll see, it's part of the problem.

Why do short-term goals seem so much easier to deal with? At least four factors jump out at us:

- It's easier to know where to start.
- It's easier to know how well we're doing.
- It's easier to know when we're done.
- It's easier to feel rewarded.

Here's a recent personal example. While I was in the middle of writing this chapter, I was asked to do a rush job of editing a book by someone else. I knew perfectly well that this book—*my* book—had a much higher priority for me. I knew that taking on the editing job would distract me from my writing and use up valuable, irreplaceable time. It didn't make any sense to agree.

Even so, like an idiot, I decided to take on the job. Why? As near as I can figure out, because:

1. The task was straightforward—putting the other guy's text into better English.
2. I could do it quickly.
3. I knew I'd be able to feel good about the job I'd done.

Oh, yes, and

4. I'd be paid for the work a lot sooner.

It's worth noticing that, in a different situation, there would have been nothing wrong with my taking the editing job. It was honest work that I enjoy and do well, and the pay wasn't terrible. In this context, however, it was taking me away from something more important but more difficult. That's typical. Very often, what we call "procrastination" is really a matter of using short-term goals as a way of avoiding longer-term goals. As long as we keep ourselves busy, we're not as likely to have to address the bothersome question of whether what we're busy at is what's most important to us.

Back in the 1930s, the humorist Robert Benchley did a comic film on the topic of how to write a magazine article. In the space of ten minutes, he found himself straightening his desk, reordering his books, and building a new bookshelf. All worthy activities, except that their obvious purpose was to put off the terrifying moment when he had to sit down, face a blank piece of paper, and start writing.

I sympathize.

How To Recognize Behavioral Traps

- Cindy learned about the risks of unsafe sex back in junior high school. But when she finds herself in a passionate embrace, the last thing on her mind is using a condom. "How can I spoil a beautiful moment?" she thinks. "You have to go with your feelings."

- Charles, who owns three dry cleaning shops, is lobbying hard to block new air pollution standards that would cost him a lot of money to comply with. An asthma sufferer, Charles admits that in the long run, the new standards might be very good for him.

- Marian wants to be fit. She's even bought a membership in a nearby health club. But there always seems to be something to do that's more attractive than exercise.

- Tony and Anna both earn good salaries, but every month more goes out than comes in. They make ends meet by writing themselves another cash advance. They've already maxed out several of their credit cards, but every time the situation starts to look dire, some bank offers them another few thousand in credit.

- Lilianne, a hairdresser, puts money aside every week toward opening her own shop. When some of her co-workers decide to try a new, expensive restaurant, she joins them and spends this week's savings.

- Sean is a field rep for a line of industrial supplies. There are a lot of small start-up companies in his region that he ought to be making contact with, but somehow he finds himself spending most of his time chewing the fat with his old familiar customers.

- Gus is a pack-a-day smoker. His uncle died of lung cancer, and his father has emphysema.

What do all these people have in common? They have all fallen victim to *behavioral traps*. In its simplest terms, a behavioral trap is a situation in which acting a particular way has a positive effect in the short run but a negative effect in the long run.

An obvious example is eating rich foods. Faced with a plate of fresh, home baked Toll House cookies, not many people have thoughts of calories, sugar, and saturated fats running through their minds. And even the few who do think about such things are likely to tell themselves, "Well, one can't hurt me." They're probably right, too. One cookie is not going to bulge out your thighs, make you hyperactive, or jam a cork in one of your coronary arteries. One drop of water isn't going to make a hole in solid rock, either, but if you've ever been to Carlsbad Caverns, you've seen what one drop of water after another can do, given enough time.

Smoking, drinking too much, and overeating are

everyday examples of what we can call *Type 1 Behavioral Traps*. They work like this:

1. You do something (smoke, drink, overeat) because the immediate feeling you get from doing it is pleasant.
2. Over the long run, the activity leads to some unpleasant consequence (health problems, social problems).

There are a number of effective ways to get out of this sort of trap, or to avoid falling into it in the first place. One is to bring some of the unpleasant consequences out of the future and into the present, for instance by posting a calorie chart and graph of your weight on the refrigerator door. Another is to develop a habit that gets in the way of the activity that has negative consequences. A friend who has a drinking problem opens a fresh diet cola every time he feels the urge to drink. By the end of the evening, he may have three or four unfinished cans of cola scattered around his apartment, but he's still sober.

Some of the best known Type 1 Behavioral Traps have given rise to self-help groups, usually modeled on the example of Alcoholics Anonymous. These groups, and the approach they take to the problems they are devoted to, are really outside the scope of this book. Information on them is widely available if you think you may need it.

Procrastination, on the other hand, is an example of a *Type 2 Behavioral Trap*. These are a little more complicated to describe (but not to understand):

1. You do something—call it *A*—that is pleasant and worthwhile in itself, but . . .

2. Doing *A* keeps you from doing something else—*B*—that is difficult, anxiety producing, or otherwise unpleasant.

3. Not doing *B* has the negative effect, in the long run, of making it harder, or even impossible, to achieve some important goal.

Sean, the sales rep who spends his time on his usual customers instead of trying to expand his clientele, has fallen into a Type 2 Behavioral Trap. Taking care of your old customers is an excellent idea—unless you're using it as a way of avoiding doing something more important but less comfortable, such as trying to make new contacts.

Here's another example of a Type 2 Trap. Imagine that you are about to be married. You'll want to be on reasonably good terms with your new spouse's family and friends, as well as your own. It's also likely that, in the weeks after the wedding, you'll have many things to do that are more urgent *and* more pleasant than writing thank you notes for the wedding presents.

We all know that, the longer you put off a thank you note, the harder it is to write. After a few months, it becomes totally impossible. You start wondering: can you get away with pretending that your note was lost in the mail? Or even pretending that the *gift* was lost in the mail? The hurt feelings of those whose gifts were never acknowledged, combined with your own awareness that you wronged them, can keep relations awkward for a very long time.

Corporate managers fall for Type 2 Behavioral

Traps, too, even if they don't call them that in business school. A big short-term profit looks good in the annual report, pleases investors, and makes your year-end bonus soar. However, the same policies that produce short-term gains may undercut long-term growth. Eventually, the cash cow runs dry and is good for nothing but hamburger.

As these examples suggest, Type 2 Behavioral Traps form a major obstacle—perhaps *the* major obstacle—to achieving our long term goals. For the rest of this chapter, we're going to look at some ways to sidestep Type 2 Traps or, if you're already caught in one, how to get out of it.

There is also a *Type 3 Behavioral Trap*, which is more social in nature. In this one:

1. People do something that is rewarding for them as individuals.

2. In the long run, the effect for people in general is negative.

A classic sad example is the Grand Banks fishery, off Newfoundland. It's clearly in each fisherman's interest to catch as many fish as he can. It's his living, after all. And the scarcer the fish become, the harder he'll work to catch more than ever. But the result of all the fishermen acting this way is that what was once one of the most productive fisheries in the world is now practically fished out.

If the coast of Newfoundland seems too remote to you, try this. Suppose you live in a crime-ridden tenement. Taking the garbage downstairs may mean taking your life in your hands. It's much safer to toss the bag out the window. And so long as you're the only one who does it, the negative effect isn't that great. But once all your neighbors start following your example. . . .

Dealing With Long Range Goals

Just a few weeks after Rudy took a job with the marketing division of a major publisher, his new boss became seriously ill. Rudy found himself handed the task of organizing the company's spring sales conference, at which top editors and authors pitch the firm's forthcoming books to the entire sales force.

Rudy knows very well that this could be a big break for him. Everyone in the corporate structure will be at the conference. There will even be representatives of the multinational that owns the company. If he does an outstanding job, he'll be noticed. If he messes up, that'll be noticed, too.

In this situation, Rudy has no problem recognizing and ordering his priorities. He has to make the conference a success. The problem is, how? He's never done anything of this sort before, there's no one in his department who can help, and the lead time he absolutely must have to do the job right is slipping through his fingers. Every time he thinks about the conference, whether it's sitting at his desk or lying awake at 3 AM, he feels completely overwhelmed. He sees his whole career going down in flames.

One part of Rudy's difficulty is that he's focussing

so much of his attention on the high cost of failure. As a result, he's like a pedestrian staring at the headlights of an oncoming truck, too caught up by the growing danger to think of ways to escape. We've already looked at some ways to deal with this sort of paralysis, in Chapter Four. As you'll recall, they include *systematic relaxation* and *blowing it up*. Rudy would be in better shape if he used one of these techniques to calm his anxiety about failure.

There's another problem, though, one that is not the result of his anxiety, but one of the sources: the *size* and *complexity* of the job. Long range goals and projects are rarely small and simple. If they were, we wouldn't have to make them long range. And the bigger and more complex they are, the more likely we are to feel overwhelmed, at a loss to know what to do.

One approach to this problem is so well known, so obvious, that I'm almost embarrassed to describe it. It's captured in a riddle that my friends and I back in fourth grade thought was a real knee-slapper:

Q: How do you eat an apple pie as big as a house?

A: One bite at a time.

Or, if you prefer proverbs, "The longest journey begins with the first step."

Notice, however, that this approach deals only with the *size* part of our problem. Whether we're talking giant pies or long hikes, the individual elements of the solution are the same. A bite's a bite, a step's a step, and the more of them you take, the closer you get to reaching your goal.

Let's imagine that I adopt this approach above to writing this book. I'd set myself quotas, a certain number of words or pages per hour, per day, per week. I'd keep careful track of how well I met my quotas. I'd draw a wall chart showing my targets and progress. And when I finished, I'd have a manuscript of 75,000 words or so, just as I'd set out to have.

What's wrong with that? Nothing, as far as it goes. But what is to say that the 75,000 words I produce are the *right* 75,000 words? I may have found a way to deal with the size aspect of my goal, but I haven't yet done anything about its complexity. That is still as overwhelming as ever.

Training a Bear

An eccentric relative has died and left you a young bear. While wondering what to do with it, you remember that you once saw a bear on tv, riding a bicycle. Aha! You are going to make a fortune by teaching *your* bear to ride a Harley-Davidson motorcycle. You can already visualize the millions in licensing fees from makers of t-shirts, kids' bedspreads, and stuffed animals. Now all you have to do is buy a motorcycle and train your bear.

So you put the bear in the back yard with the Harley, but after a few sniffs, the bear decides that it's more fun to sharpen its claws on your cedar siding. When you try riding in circles, the bear watches but shows no sign of wanting to imitate you. Even repeated playings of "Leader of the Pack" do no good. Your morale rapidly sinks toward zero.

Faced with this challenge, a skilled, professional animal trainer would probably make use of the technique behavioral psychologists call *shaping*. This involves taking a complicated activity and breaking it down into simpler elements that can be more easily learned and performed.

We might start by training the bear to go over to the motorcycle. Next, we teach it to climb on and sit while the kickstand is down. Once that's well in place, we have it sit while the bike is moving slowly and we run alongside to steer. And so on, until the day that Brother Bruin shows up for work in a black leather jacket with an eagle on the back. It may not be easy, but in time shaping can train animals to do things that to anyone else look miraculous.

To return to Rudy, he could organize his spring sales conference according to the underlying principle of shaping:

> When a long range goal seems so big and complicated that you feel overwhelmed, break it down into smaller, simpler steps.

Of course, some projects make this easier to do than others. For instance, the thought of writing an entire book is pretty daunting for anyone, even an experienced author. However, books are generally organized in chapters, and very often the chapters are organized in sections and subsections. The "smaller, simpler steps" are already there waiting for you.

Rudy's task is a little harder. He has to think through the different aspects of holding a conference, then break each of those into doable chunks. But once he starts, he's likely to find that some of the work is done for him.

"But I Don't Know Where To Start!"

Anywhere.

That's right, anywhere. What's important is not *where* you start, but *that* you start. If you wait until your plans are perfected, you may never move out of the starting gate. And even if you did, once you got going you'd probably discover that you needed to make some changes in those carefully perfected plans anyway.

Back in the days when many more people smoked, my older brother taught me a game to play for drinks. You stretch a tissue or paper napkin over the mouth of a beer mug and place a dime in the center. Then each person around the table takes a turn at touching the lit end of a cigarette to the paper. Soon, only a charred, lacy web is holding up the dime. The person who burns the hole that makes the coin fall into the mug buys the next round.

When you think about trying to achieve a long-term goal, remember that paper napkin. Every hole you burn in it—wherever it is, however tiny it may be—brings you a little closer to the moment when the dime drops. But in this case, that means that you *win* the game.

So Rudy might start by a) getting the list of forthcoming books, b) noting which editor is responsible for each book, c) drafting a lively invitation to the sales force, and d) having a preliminary phone chat with the convention manager at the hotel. He could probably get all that done before lunch, without breaking a sweat. And as he went along, each step would suggest other steps.

You can start by doing the following exercise. Don't agonize over your answers. Try to let your ideas flow, without censoring them in advance. The whole exercise shouldn't take you more than ten or fifteen minutes.

Goals and Steps

1. For me, an important long range goal is

2. Achieving this goal will involve, among other things,

   A.

   B.

   C.

   D.

3. Some small, simple steps I can take toward accomplishing *A* through *D* are

   _____ _____

   _____ _____

   _____ _____

   _____ _____

   _____ _____

   _____ _____

   _____ _____

Now, go through all the steps you wrote down in section 3 and circle *every one that you think you can do in fifteen minutes or less.*

Think of it as playing a trick on yourself. Most of us see ourselves as too busy just taking care of what's urgent and immediate to deal with long range goals. We don't have the time, we don't have the energy. But I am willing to bet that at some point in the next day or two, you will find yourself with fifteen minutes to spare. When the moment comes, whip out that list of steps toward your long range goal and *do one of them.*

Which one? You could easily waste those fifteen minutes just trying to decide. Don't! If you like to think of yourself as the methodical sort, choose the one that happens to be at the top of the list. If you're more comfortable with the image of a wild and crazy guy, shade your eyes and stab the list with your pencil.

If few, or none, of the items on your list can be done in fifteen minutes, then go through it again and list still smaller, simpler steps. Let's say you have a goal of getting control of your finances, and this involves organizing your financial records. You know from experience that that would eat up at least a whole day, so it never gets done. You're almost at the point of buying a new pair of shoes, just so you'll have another shoebox for those important papers.

Okay, break it down into smaller, simpler tasks. Spend no more than fifteen minutes sorting your bank statements into this year's, last year's, and those that date back to the Eisenhower Administration. During your next fifteen minute stint, go through that carton of documents, pull out any tax returns you come across, and stick them in a *labeled* file folder. You won't find them all first time through, but at least you'll know where *some* of them are. Before you know it, you'll be more organized than not, and the piles of unsorted papers will look small enough to deal with in one sitting.

Of course, that list of fifteen minute steps is of no use if you don't look at it. One friend of mine, who spends the greater part of every day in front of his Macintosh, has a simple program that puts little color-coded notes, like electronic Post-its, on the screen. He can easily edit them, move them around, add to them, and put them in the trash. While he's working on something else, they're hidden, but whenever he has a few spare moments, a single mouse click brings up the list.

Or you could do as another friend does. He writes each different task on a piece of paper and keeps them in a box on his desk. Whenever he has a little free time, he reaches in and does whichever one he pulls out. Think of it as activity roulette. Or use any other method you're comfortable with. What's important is to get past choosing and on to doing.

When you do, you'll make the surprising discovery that working toward your goal isn't quite as overwhelming as it seemed. Inertia begins to work for you instead of against you. In Jack London's classic novel, *The Call of the Wild*, Buck, the dog who is the hero of the book, has to pull a heavily loaded sled a hundred yards. His master has bet everything he has that Buck will succeed. London describes in heartbreaking detail the dog's excruciating effort to get the sled moving. For a long while, it seems certain that he'll fail. But once Buck succeeds in getting the sled in motion, its momentum makes his task a little easier with every step.

One problem with this approach is that it doesn't make enough use of forethought. If you're packing for a long trip and you simply throw things in the suitcase as they occur to you, whatever you need the first night always ends up at the bottom. It's a well-known law of nature. But what if, instead, you toss them on the bed? You're still putting together what you need, without all those long agonies over what to select next. And once the pile on the bed looks big enough, you can organize it as you pack.

That's right, organize it. Because, sooner or later, logic and organization do have to come into play. At some point, Rudy will have to sit down, try to list all the necessary preparations for the conference he's organizing, and make sure that he's taken care of them. If I really were to move to France, the time would come when I'd have to confront visas, bank accounts, health insurance, and what to do with all those cartons of books in the basement. As you take more and more steps toward your long-term goal, you'll reach a place where you have to pause and carefully chart your next moves.

By the time that happens, you'll discover that you've already accomplished a surprising amount. And that will make what remains to be done look much less overwhelming.

Rewards Along the Way

Earlier in this chapter, we looked at four reasons that short term goals seem so much easier to deal with than long term goals. The fourth reason was, *It's easier to feel rewarded*, because it's built into the situation. The reward comes when you accomplish your aim. If your aim will take months or years to accomplish, who could blame you if you get tired of the delay in being rewarded and decide to go for something less fulfilling but more accessible?

A few years ago, my brother-in-law, who is a behavioral psychologist, produced an educational film about a rat named Barnabas. In the opening sequence, Barnabas scampers confidently through a Rube Goldberg construction, climbing ladders, negotiating twisty passages, even pulling himself across a rickety bridge on a little cable car. Once at the top, Barnabas steps onto the platform of an elevator, tugs at a string that hoists an American flag, and returns to ground level to receive his reward, a tasty pellet of rat chow. It's an amazing performance.

The rest of the film shows how Barnabas was taught this routine. The technique that was used is called *backward chaining*. This involves starting at the end of the line and working backwards. Barnabas first learned that there was food in the goal box. The next lesson was that, if he pressed a certain lever, he'd be rewarded by getting to the *door* of the goal box. Getting to the *lever* was the reward for the next action he learned. By the end of the training, Barnabas had learned the entire complicated sequence of steps. For each of these steps, the reward was the chance to perform the *next* step, until at last he reached the goal box and the food.

There are some obvious differences between Barnabas's situation and ours. He is learning a chain of actions that he will perform many times, once he's got it down. What we're trying to do is get ourselves to perform a chain of actions that, if it works, we'll probably never perform again. Whatever your long range goal—starting your own business, slimming down to your ideal weight, getting your master's degree—I doubt if you really want to do it more than once. You want to reach it and move on.

However, the basic principle that underlies the training of Barnabas is one that is immensely valuable for us, too.

> To maintain the level of motivation needed to reach a long range goal, *bring the rewards of achieving the future goal back into the present.*

When you make a move in the direction of your long range goal, give yourself something. This can be something material (a special snack, a trip to the pool), something psychological (a self-administered pat on the back), or both at the same time.

Earlier I suggested you draw up a list of steps toward your goal. If you did, did you then follow it? Now as you accomplish a step and check it off, make it into a production. Use a fat red marker. Play a tape of a trumpet fanfare. Call up a friend and ask for congratulations. You deserve them. Before, you were letting yourself drift, pushed one way and another by the immediate and the urgent. No longer. Now you've chosen your own destination and started to steer a course toward it.

7

WORK AND PLAY

When my daughter was a baby, one of her favorite toys was a plastic panel with an assortment of knobs, latches, buttons, and levers. I suspect it's one of the best-selling baby toys around. I know that our pediatrician keeps two or three of them in the waiting room, and they are always in use. A few minutes spent watching a little kid playing with one would show you why.

Look at that intent expression. You know right away that this isn't idle twiddling. It's serious business. Manipulating some of the knobs and latches may be a struggle, but the challenge only makes the child work at it harder. And when moving a lever produces a rachety noise or pushing a button makes a little door spring open, you'll see a wide smile and hear a crow of delight.

The renowned Swiss child psychologist, Jean Piaget, said that children are born with a built-in desire to explore. They naturally want to try out new things, to understand, and to gain mastery over the world around them. When a two-year-old manages to fit a smaller cup into a larger one, or stack blocks four

164

high, or do a wobbly approximation of a somersault, the joy she feels comes *from within*. She probably won't even bother to look around for praise from others. And if the blocks fall down—or she does—she'll either try again or move on to some other game, without any great upset.

What's true of the two-year-old is—or at least was—true of all of us. Once upon a time, you and I also had that urge to seek out challenges, just for the joy of mastering them.

Now look at the people around you, in your office, factory, or classroom. How many are deeply, joyfully involved in what they are doing? How many, on the other hand, are bored and alienated, dragging themselves through their daily routine?

You know the answer. In the words of an old labor union song:

> We go to work, to earn the money
> To buy the bread, to get the strength
> To go to work, to earn the money
> To buy the bread, to get the strength . . .

What on earth happened to us? What became of that curiosity, that inner motivation that Piaget talked about? Did we simply outgrow it? Did we somehow lose it? Or is it still somewhere within us, but kept hidden by other factors in our personality and environment? And if it isn't lost for good, how can we revive it and give it back the central role it once had?

Those are urgent questions for all of us. They bear directly on the quality of our lives. In this chapter, we'll try to answer them.

What Makes It Work?

HELP WANTED—seasonal outdoor work in severe weather conditions. Heavy physical demands. Must relocate to remote area. Hours dawn to dusk. Risk of serious work-related injuries. Must supply own tools and work clothes. Minimal pay, no benefits, no job security. Apply. . . .

What would it take to get you to try for that job? How desperate would you have to be? Do you think they'd have any takers at all?

Now suppose I fill in the words at the end, after the three dots: *Snow Mountain Ski Resort, Winterland, Vermont.* Does that change your opinion?

"No fair!" you say. "A job at a ski resort? They must have applicants lining up around the block. But that's because it's not really work."

Why not? The job description *is* accurate, and it certainly *sounds* like work. What changed your mind? Consider these examples as well:

- Debbie, a systems analyst with a Fortune 500 company, devotes her weekends, and lots of evenings after work, to golf. She saves up during the year so that she can spend her vacation near a famous golf course. She likes watching tournament play but has no desire to compete herself.

- Marco has studied oboe since the age of twelve. While earning a master's degree at the conservatory, he started playing with two chamber groups. He teaches privately and at a local music school, and practices at least four

hours a day. Last year, when a regional or-
chestra had an opening for an oboist, Marco
was one of over a hundred players to audition.
Though the judges were very impressed with
his performance, they didn't pick him.

- Justin, a junior in college, cracks the books
just enough to keep his grades at an acceptable
level. The rest of his time is dedicated to computer games. When a new one comes out, he
can't rest until he has mastered every level.
He recently started his own 'zine on the World
Wide Web, giving tips and hints about his favorite games.

- Marcella does data entry during the day and
waits tables evenings and weekends to pay for
her acting, voice, fencing, and dance classes.
She and three friends hope to put on a show-
case production this spring, if they can raise
the money, and she is being considered by
several summer stock companies.

- Peter, a psychotherapist, has a completely
equipped cabinetmaking shop in his basement,
where he makes replicas of museum-quality
Early American furniture. He often spends as
much as several months on a single piece.

If you were to measure the amount of time, energy,
and concentration that these people devote to their
favored activities, it would probably be more than
most of us put into our regular jobs. Yet something
makes us shy away from calling what they do *work*.

We can get one hint of what that is from the way
we speak about them. Debbie *plays* golf, Marco *plays*
the oboe, Justin *plays* computer games, and Marcella

plays roles in *plays*, when she gets the chance. Peter is odd man out, but his furnituremaking would be called a *hobby*, a word that has close ties to the idea of play.

Why do we say that somebody plays golf, but not that he or she plays business? (I know—sometimes we say that a person plays *at* business, but it's never meant as a compliment.) Seriousness? Many golfers take their performance at least as seriously as many businesspeople. Productivity? Hitting a little white ball around a big park may not do much to raise the world's standard of living, but does it do any less than the average lawsuit?

Intrinsic and Extrinsic Rewards

One thing Debbie, Michael, and the others have in common is that *because* they enjoy what they do, they want to keep doing it. That may not sound like a strong candidate for Revelation of the Year, but it does point us toward a more general idea:

The more we see ourselves doing something for *extrinsic* reasons, the more we think of the activity as *work*.

The more we see ourselves doing something for *intrinsic* reasons (''for its own sake''), the less we think of the activity as work and the more we think of it as *play*.

An ''extrinsic'' reason is one that *isn't* built in, that comes from outside the activity itself. For example, doing something to get money. Unless you're a gold prospector or a counterfeiter, money isn't a natural, direct result of your work. It's a social consequence. You do something that other people want you to do, and they pay you in return.

Doing something to avoid punishment is extrinsic, too. If it weren't for the threat of punishment, we wouldn't do it. Do you remember what it felt like to write a book report that had to be in the next morning and had to be at least 150 words long, *or else*? How much did you enjoy reading the book and writing about it? How much real, creative thought went into your report? How many times did you count each word, hoping that somehow you had reached the magic number?

Getting social approval, keeping up with the neighbors, keeping your boss from getting on your case, winning a promotion, or simply holding onto your job ... the list of possible extrinsic reasons for doing something can be as long as you want to make it.

Doing things for intrinsic reasons differs in that the rewards are *built into* the activity. There's a challenge in it, a chance to use our skills and abilities.

- If you're a crossword fan, you get pleasure from each tricky clue you manage to figure out.

- If you're a runner, you get pleasure from the movement, from the sensation of muscles working efficiently, from the passing scene, from the feeling that you are using your body as it is meant to be used.

- If you're a lawyer, you get pleasure from finding a way through an intricate case or discovering an obscure but relevant precedent.

- And we all remember what the great alpinist,

Mallory, said, when asked why he wanted to climb Everest: "Because it is there."

Even when two people are involved in the same activity, one may experience it as work and another as play. Look at the expressions in the exercise room of a health club. They range from grin to grim. Some people are clearly enjoying themselves. Others, maybe even at the next machine, are obviously doing it because they feel they have to and can't wait to finish.

Once, when my daughter was about three, I started blowing bubbles to entertain her. It worked, too. She was obviously having great fun chasing and popping them. As I went on, though, I was intrigued to discover that by wetting my lips, then blowing a very soft, very steady stream of air, I could produce much bigger bubbles. My daughter didn't care a bit whether the bubbles were big or small. She just wanted to run after and catch them. But *I* cared. My motivation had changed, in a more intrinsic direction. For the next few minutes, I was personally involved, caught up in the challenge of blowing bigger bubbles.

This incident leads to an important point. Our reasons for doing something can change as we go along. We may start doing something for extrinsic reasons, then discover that it has intrinsic rewards. A child who goes to his music lessons and does his practicing for no other reason than that he's told he has to may realize after a while that he enjoys playing and wants to go on studying. We may also start doing something for intrinsic reasons, then lose sight of those reasons and pay attention only to extrinsic reasons.

It's also possible to do something for both intrinsic and extrinsic reasons. In that case, what really matters is which reasons seem more important to you.

Carol bought her first camera when she was fourteen. Since then, she has seemed to spend every spare moment either taking pictures or improving her darkroom skills. Every spare cent goes to upgrading her equipment. In recent months, she has been thinking more and more seriously about leaving her day job and turning full-time professional.

Lately, she has done some challenging and profitable photo assignments for magazines. These jobs take a lot of hard effort, but when she finishes, her favorite way to relax is to reload her cameras and go out again. When a friend asks her why, she says, "I love taking pictures, that's all. It's terrific that people will pay me to do it, but believe me, if I had to, *I'd pay them!*"

Choice and Constraint

That half hour or so I spent blowing bubbles has another important implication for us. I didn't experience what I was doing as *work*. I was having fun. True, the source of my fun—the delight I saw on my daughter's face—came from outside the activity itself. And you could say that she, and her reactions, were controlling what I did. I *chose*, however, to put myself in that position. I *wanted* to have fun with her. If I hadn't, I could have plopped her down in front of some crayons and paper or a pile of Legos or the TV. In fact, I still could have done that at any point, if my own efforts to keep her amused had stopped working. I had options, and I had the power to select among them.

Suppose I work full time in a day care center. I like kids, but that's not the main reason I'm there. I'm there because, with my qualifications and given the state of the economy, it's the best option available to me. During my hours there, I *have* to see that the kids are entertained, occupied, or at least reasonably quiet. If I don't manage to do it, the director gets on my back. And if I still can't do it, I find myself out on the street.

Am I having fun? Do my activities bring me a feeling of joy and fulfillment? Or do I mostly focus on simply trying to get through the day? And what makes the difference? The answer is that I'm doing what I do because I have to, not because I want to. To put it more formally:

> The more we see ourselves as *choosing* to do something, the more internally motivated we are to do it.
>
> The more we see ourselves as being *constrained* to do something, the less internally motivated we are to do it.

An internal motivation shows itself in several important ways.

- We look for opportunities to do it.
- When we find one, we're eager to get started.
- While we're doing it, we feel interested and involved.
- When we run into obstacles, we keep trying.
- If something or someone stops us from doing it, we feel frustrated and angry.

Hobbies are an obvious example. We look forward to making time for them, we spend hard-earned cash on equipment and materials, we lose track of time when we're engaged in them. But an internally motivated activity doesn't have to be a hobby, and the personal cost of pursuing it may be very steep. I'm thinking of a young man who went to Somalia with a voluntary relief organization. While he was there, most of one leg was blown off by a land mine. After half a dozen major operations and months in a rehabilitation program, he signed up with an organization that is trying to curb the international traffic in land mines.

You're more likely to get it done if you are internally motivated to do it. And you're more internally motivated to do it if you have chosen to do it.

What *You* Choose to Do

In this section, you'll have a chance to look more closely at some of your own activities and see which are primarily internally motivated and which are primarily externally motivated. You should be able to finish this questionnaire in fifteen minutes or less.

First, write down some activities that are (a) job-related, and (b) non-job-related. These don't have to be the most important or most frequent, as long as they are what spring to your mind when you think about your work or leisure. For example, when I think of my work at the university, the activities that first come to mind are teaching, attending department meetings, and grading exams and papers.

I've provided three blanks in each category, but you don't have to stop at three if you're motivated to consider more.

Once you've made your list of activities, think about each in turn. Ask yourself two questions:

> To what extent do I do this because I have to?
>
> To what extent do I do this because I want to?

Notice that these questions aren't automatic opposites. I teach my classes both because I have to *and* because I want to. I'm writing this chapter both because I want to and because I have a deadline that's coming up all too quickly.

As an aid to answering the questions, think of them this way: If you had no desire at all to do this activity, how much would you feel you had to do it anyway? If nothing at all were forcing you to do it, how much would you want to do it anyway?

To answer each question, put an X somewhere along the line under the question, at the place that comes closest to the way you feel.

ACTIVITIES, CONSTRAINT, AND CHOICE

JOB-RELATED ACTIVITIES

1. <u>Data entry related</u>

    I do this because I *have to*:

    never   sometimes   always

    I do this because I *want to*:

    never   sometimes   always

2. <u>Teaching something on comp.</u>

    I do this because I *have to*:

    never   sometimes   always

    I do this because I *want to*:

    never   sometimes   always

3. <u>Brainstorm ideas for better buss</u>

    I do this because I *have to*:

    never   sometimes   always

    I do this because I *want to*:

    never   sometimes   always

NON-JOB-RELATED ACTIVITIES

1. ___Read_____

I do this because I *have to*:

<----------X--------------------------->
never   sometimes   always
I do this because I *want to*:

<-------------------------------X------->
never   sometimes   always

2. ___Write in journal_____

I do this because I *have to*:

<--X------------------------------------>
never   sometimes   always
I do this because I *want to*:

<-------------------------------X------->
never   sometimes   always

3. ___Update planner_____

I do this because I *have to*:

<-------------------X------------------->
never   sometimes   always
I do this because I *want to*:

<-------------------------------X------->
never   sometimes   always

You can tell a lot about your attitudes by simply looking at where you placed your X's. If you want a more precise measure, here's how to get it:

1. Each line is broken up into seven intervals. The interval over "never" gets a score of one, the interval over "sometimes" gets a score of four, and the interval over "always" gets a score of seven. In the margin next to each line, write the score of the interval your X is in. If you put your X right over the dot between two intervals, give it the higher score.

2. For each of the activities you rated, subtract the "want to" score from the "have to" score. The result can range anywhere between +6 and −6.

   a score of +4, +5, or +6 means that the activity is *strongly* motivated by external reasons

   a score of +2 or +3 means that the activity is *weakly* motivated by external reasons

   a score of +1, 0, or −1 means that the activity is motivated *equally* by external and internal reasons

   a score of −2 or −3 means that the activity is *weakly* motivated by internal reasons

   a score of −4, −5, or −6 means that the activity is *strongly* motivated by internal reasons

Bonus or Discount?

In scoring the answers on the questionnaire, we
subtracted one kind of motivation—"want to," or internal—from the other—"have to," or external. Why
didn't we add them up, instead? Isn't it better to have
both kinds of motivation operating? If there's something you have to do anyway, then isn't also wanting
to do it a kind of bonus?

Sometimes, yes, but all too often we run afoul of
what social psychologists call the *discounting principle*:

> The more we think that we're doing something
> for *external* reasons, the *less* weight we give to
> our *internal* motivation.

Do you remember the books you had to read for high
school and college English? Chances are, at least
some of them were books you would have enjoyed
reading if a friend had recommended them. But because you knew you were reading them for an external reason, you probably *discounted* the amount of
pleasure you got from reading them. You looked on
it as work, not play.

The discounting principle operates when we look
at what other people do, too. Say a senator attacks
a particular record company for the violent lyrics of
some of its songs. If you then find out that he received a big campaign contribution from a rival record company, you'll probably *discount* his personal
reasons for making the attack and decide it's "all
politics."

Consider this:

As part of their Introductory Psychology class, Jeremy and Steve signed up to take part in a research project on problem-solving strategies.

When Jeremy arrived at the lab, the researcher showed him some interesting, challenging puzzles and asked him to spend twenty minutes on them. She explained that he would be paid $5 for each one he solved. When the twenty minutes were up, he was shown to a waiting room, where there were some magazines and some of the puzzles. After another length of time, he was thanked, paid, and told he could go.

Steve, too, spent twenty minutes on the puzzles, then waited in the waiting room. His experience was exactly the same as Jeremy's, with one crucial difference. At no point did the researcher even hint that he might be paid for solving the puzzles.

This situation is modeled after a series of experiments by psychologist Edward Deci, of the University of Rochester. It wasn't until afterwards that the participants learned what the researchers were really interested in. During the period that they spent in the waiting room, a hidden observer had been watching them, measuring how much of their *free time* they spent on the puzzles.

In study after study, the results have turned out the same. The people in one of the groups spent more of their waiting time on the puzzles than those in the other group. Can you figure out which one? Ordinarily, we'd reason that if both groups did the same interesting puzzles, and one group got paid as well, that group would come away with a more positive attitude toward the activity. So when they had another chance to spend time on the puzzles, they'd be more likely to take advantage of it. What that reasoning leaves out, however, is the discounting principle.

Ask yourself: What did the experience *feel like* to the people who took part? Why did they think they were doing it?

For one group—the *unpaid* group—they were spending twenty minutes trying to solve some intriguing puzzles, because the puzzles were intriguing. So when, in the waiting room, they had the opportunity to go on playing with the puzzles, they took it.

But the other group—the *paid* group—saw that they were being paid to solve the puzzles. That led them to *discount* the amount of fun they had doing it. They began to see it more as a job. So later, in the waiting room, when they knew that they wouldn't be paid to work on the puzzles, they didn't.

Turning Play Into Work

I just noticed that, in the last section, my vocabulary changed as I went from talking about one of the groups to talking about the other. Did you notice, too? I described the paid group as *working on* the puzzles and the unpaid group as *playing with* the puzzles, even though they were both doing the same puzzles. That's a good example of the discounting principle in operation.

Here's another:

In one of my courses, I was describing the research you just read about. As I finished, I noticed one of the students, a young man with a long ponytail and two earrings. He looked stunned, almost glassy-eyed. I asked him if he was okay.

He blinked and said, "This is so weird! I'm a musician, right? That's like been my whole life since I was a kid. My best friends and I are in a band. We get together in one guy's basement practically every day to rehearse."

"Um-hum?" I said, when he seemed to be winding down. I already suspected where he was headed.

He frowned in concentration. "Well," he said slowly, "things are really looking up for us. It's fantastic. We're getting gigs, we're in talks with an agent, the A&R guy for a record company asked for our demo tape. I should be flying. And I am, some of the time. But other times I catch myself thinking weird thoughts. Like, rehearsals are a drag. Gigs are a drag. The whole bit is a drag. This is what I've lived to do for years, and now it's turning into a drag. And I think I see why. It's not *my* music anymore, it's a job!"

That's what is so insidious about the effect of the discounting principle. It leads us to overlook or downplay our own internal motives for doing something, and to focus too much on the external reasons. We take what could have felt like play, and we experience it as work.

Have you ever spent a family vacation at the seaside? From the moment they wake up, the kids are clamoring to go to the beach. But if you decide you'd like some time alone and you try to *send* them to the beach, forget it. It's too sunny, or too cloudy; the water's too warm, or too cold; there's nothing to do there anyway. By taking away their sense of *choosing* to go, you make them forget that they *want* to go.

The discounting principle operates even when we create the external reasons ourselves. For example, lots of people try to keep their projects on track by setting deadlines for themselves. That's fine, as long as you see the deadline as a way of knowing how far along you are. But the moment you start "working to meet the deadline," you run the risk of undercutting your internal motivation to do the job. You may still get it done, but you probably won't do it as well. You certainly won't enjoy doing it as much.

The difference can be very subtle. When I start on a writing project, I usually make a chart that shows what needs to be done and the amount of time I have to do it in. For years, I would next take a ruler and draw a line from the starting point, in the lower left hand corner, to the finishing point, in the upper right hand corner. So many pages a day, and I'd easily finish on time. Then as I went along, I'd mark in each day's progress on the chart.

This schedule sounds like a fine idea, the type of advice you hear all the time from management experts. In my case, however, I noticed it was having a bad effect on me. Like a lot of projects, mine generally start off slow and gradually build momentum. The result was that, according to the chart, I was *always behind*.

Meeting the quota became the focus of my day's work. When I succeeded, all I felt was a sense of relief, and when—as happened more often—I didn't, the needle on my mood meter stuck somewhere between grim and desperate. I gradually forgot that the project was something I had freely chosen to do, and started to see it as something I *had* to do.

Once I realized what was going on, I made one simple change. I still make a progress chart, but I *don't* draw that quota line on it. Now, when I mark in a day's work, what I see is how much I've accomplished, not how far off I am from what I was *supposed* to accomplish.

"But I Need Deadlines!"

That's a feeling I know very well. You go along for days or weeks, telling yourself that you're mulling over a project, doing creative thinking. You even make a few notes to yourself. Then, the night before it's due, you sit down at your desk and realize that you're still at square one. Panic time! You make a pot of coffee, pop a couple of wake-up pills, and put everything you've got into it. By four in the morning, your shirt is wringing wet, your eyes keep crossing, and you've got a crew with jackhammers going at your temples, but the project is finished.

Dr. Johnson put it best, over two hundred years ago: "Depend upon it, Sir, the prospect of being hanged in a fortnight concentrates a man's faculties wonderfully."

Now you've got it done. You wander around your office filled with grim pride, muttering "When the going gets tough, the tough get going." You wish you could wear a medal on your chest that reads, *Hero Worker*. You want everyone to know what you've done.

But was it fun?

And what will happen the next time you have something that has to be done? You'll remember the agony of that last minute push, the lack of any positive feeling except sheer relief that it was behind you, and you'll put off the new project as long as you can. Is it any wonder that you start feeling as though you have a knapsack full of bricks strapped to your back?

What if you hadn't gotten it done, or don't next time? We all know what "deadline" means—cross the line on time, or you're dead. Not literally, I hope, but the sense of futility, incompetence, and despair that flow from your failure may make you *wish* you were dead.

Constraint works, of course. The bullwhip and the bowl of soup are the oldest management tools around. They were used to build the Pyramids, fling a net of roads over the Roman Empire, wall off the northern border of China, dig the mines that fueled the Industrial Revolution. But at what a cost, not just to the people who did the work, but to the end product as well. Forced labor is grudging labor, and it shows.

That's so even when we're forcing ourselves. When I *choose* to cook dinner, I think about what dishes would go well together, I put care into the preparation, I try to present the food in an interesting, attractive way. When I tell myself that I *have* to cook dinner, it's edible, it's nutritious, it takes me just as much work, but there's something sad and lifeless about the result.

Playing to Win Is Work

Olympic athletes go for the gold. Politicians vie for their party's presidential nomination. Law partners try to amass the highest billings in the firm. PTA members strive to send the fanciest contribution to the annual bake sale. Little boys stand in a row and see who can pee the farthest. Wherever we look, people are involved in *competition*.

And competition can seem to do wonders for your motivation.

- You're taking a leisurely bike ride through the park when some kid zips past you and makes a rude noise. Without even thinking, you pick up the pace and set off after him.

- As you make the rounds of your customers, you discover that in each place, the new rep for a rival company has gotten there ahead of you. You start scheduling more appointments per day and taking shorter lunch breaks.

- At a party, you notice someone attractive hitting on your date. You become livelier and more attentive.

In each of these situations, you are in *direct competition* with someone. You're struggling against the other person, trying both to maximize your successes *and* to minimize your rival's. These are also examples of what games theorists call *zero-sum games*. The more I win, the more you lose, and vice-versa. Whether we're talking about tennis, chess, or a battle for market share, a victory for you is a defeat for me.

Both the joy of winning and the pain of losing can be powerful motivators. No one would argue with that. But, like powerful medications, they should be used cautiously, after a careful look at the possible side effects. These include:

- *Discounting*—the more we see ourselves as doing something in order to win, the less weight we'll give to our other, more internal reasons for doing it.

- *Face-saving*—to increase our chances of winning, we may avoid real challenges and instead choose easier tasks and opponents.

- *Withdrawal*—if we see the rewards of winning as our main reason for doing the activity, we're likely to get discouraged and drop out if we *don't* win.

- *Emotionality*—the arousal that's generated in a competitive setting makes it more likely that we'll get emotional, lose our temper, and act aggressively.

We can often get more intense performance through competition, but because of these side effects, sometimes there is a high cost.

Look at a bunch of kids playing a pickup game of sandlot baseball, then look at the same kids playing for a Little League title. Maybe the play in the pickup game is a little sloppier, but it is clearly *play*. The kids are having fun, and if the winners feel a little better than the losers at the end, the losers still feel good about the game. Why shouldn't they? Their most important goal was to play, and they achieved that.

Notice the difference between their experience and that of the team in the championship, whose most important goal is to win. The grim expressions on the faces of the team that's behind, the way those who are ahead make fun of those who are behind, the anger and tears when the game is over—this is supposed to be *fun*?

One of the most insidious effects of a purely competitive attitude is the way it can warp and stunt our own development. We've seen that real personal growth comes through tackling challenges that are neither too easy nor too hard for us. But if your aim is not growing but winning, you don't want a challenge, you want a lead-pipe cinch.

You *can* benefit from competition without undermining your intrinsic motivation for what you're doing, if certain conditions are met:

- The external rewards of winning and penalties of losing are not the most important aspect of the activity.
- The competition is tough enough to challenge you but not to overwhelm you.
- You focus on what the activity and the outcome can tell you about your skills and approach.

A closely fought point in tennis or a closely fought game of chess can be almost as exhilarating if you lose as if you win. Losing a big contract or an important promotion, on the other hand, will never be fun. But if you pay close attention to what the experience tells you about your own strong and weak points, you can convert its negative impact into a positive, growth-promoting force.

Painting the Picket Fence

Do you remember the story of Tom Sawyer and the fence? Mark Twain's boy hero is about to enjoy a carefree Saturday morning. Then his Aunt Polly tells him that he has to whitewash the picket fence. He is sure that his day is ruined. As he starts to paint the fence, he comes up with a wonderfully clever plan. When his friends come by, he pretends to be having great fun. His friends, fooled, beg him to let them join in. They even offer him bribes for a turn with the whitewash brush.

I imagine that most people who read that episode come away thinking how shrewd Tom was and how gullible his friends were. I know I did. Now, however, I see it in a very different light: Tom *didn't* dupe his friends. They really did have fun painting the fence. *What was a chore to Tom was a game to them.*

Why? Wasn't it exactly the same activity for him and them? No, it wasn't. The physical activity—dipping the brush into the pail of whitewash, spreading it over the fence—was the same, but not the way they thought about it. Tom concentrated on the external reason he was doing it, that his aunt had ordered him to. He disregarded any sense of accomplishment, physical pleasure, or other internal satisfaction that he might have gotten from doing it. But his friends were freely *choosing* to paint the fence. There was no external pressure forcing them to do it. For them, only the internal reasons counted.

This story gives us a valuable clue to solving the mystery we started this chapter with. How did we lose our innate pleasure in trying things out and mastering them? How did adventure turn into drudgery? And most important, is there still a road back?

Some lucky few don't seem to need a road back, because they never left. Whether they are artists priming a new canvas, gardeners naturalizing a new variety of rose, or executives structuring a synergistic corporate merger, they all have certain characteristics in common:

- They search out new challenges and approach them with anticipation.

- They come up with new, creative answers to problems.

- They persist even when the rest of the world treats what they're doing with indifference or scorn.

- They learn what they can from their failures, then move on to new challenges.

- Above all, they take pleasure from the activity itself.

If you were to ask these people what their secret is, they'd probably give you a baffled look. There is no secret. They're just leading their lives in what seems to them like the normal, natural way. For them, the puzzle is not why they are the way they are, but why *everyone* isn't that way.

However, we are now in a position to say what makes them different. What they do may bring them fame and fortune, or leave them in poverty and neglect, but either way, they go on seeing and appreciating the *intrinsic rewards* the activity brings them. They may be under strong external pressure to go on with the activity, they may even depend on it for life's necessities, but they never forget that ultimately they are doing it by their own *choice*.

Somehow they have kept their thoughts and feelings from being distorted by the discounting principle.

What they do naturally,
we can do deliberately.

Turning Work Into Play

Now that we understand the factors that changed
what we once liked to do into something we do grudg-
ingly at best, we can start trying to reverse the process. We can uncover long-buried sources of
enthusiasm and joy in our daily lives, and we can
begin to reshape our thinking to give those sources
more of the importance they deserve. And you don't
have to change your whole life, either.

You don't have to do anything radical or irrevers-
ible. The change that matters most is internal. It's a
question of altering the way you think about and experience what you do. Once that process is under way,
you *may* choose to make changes in the way you lead
your life as well. You may decide to take your shot
at a long-deferred dream, or to make a profession of
a hobby you're passionate about. Or you may go on
doing exactly what you've always done, but with a
new spirit and outlook.

Our starting point is one simple fact:

Much of what we do has, or can have, intrinsic
as well as extrinsic rewards.

Suppose you make your living repairing appliances,
a job that offers you many intrinsic rewards. You
meet a lot of people, you're always on the move, you
get to work with your hands, you get pride from your
ability to spot and fix common problems quickly, now

and then you stumble on a problem that's a real brain-teaser. It may not be Paradise, it is still a job, but there's a lot to be said for it. There's a lot to be said for *your* job, too, if you look at it the right way.

The same is true for everyday chores. My wife claims to *like* washing dishes. She says it gives her a chance to relax and let her mind drift. I can't say I like washing dishes, but I put up with it by making it into a game. The object is to finish up with the dishes sorted by size in the drying rack. You may think that sounds a little peculiar, but for me it keeps the process mildly interesting. That's a big improvement over bored resentment.

Resentment is one of the most common reactions to feeling put upon, whether by your boss, your parents, your husband or wife, Uncle Sam, or life itself. You may love to sing, but if someone *insists* that you sing, someone you think you can't say no to, you'll probably do it resentfully, because you feel put upon. Your right to choose has been taken away.

But has it really? Suppose you said to yourself, "I'm about to do something I usually like to do. True, the circumstances aren't what I would have chosen. Still, it's a chance to do something that I know holds intrinsic rewards for me. Therefore, I choose to do it and get as much out of it as I can."

As you go through the next few days, pick at least three significant activities that you *don't* look forward to doing, but do anyway. I'd suggest that two of them be job-related and the third more personal. As we did in Chapter Five, we're going to look at three elements:

- an ACTIVITY—what you do
- an ATTRIBUTION—why you feel you do it

- an ARGUMENT—some other, more intrinsic, rewards that you might find in the activity.

Here's an example:

ACTIVITY

I . . . *gave my boss a progress report on a project he asked me to keep an eye on.*

ATTRIBUTION

I did this because . . . *I have to prove to him that I can handle bigger responsibilities if I want to have a real future with the company.*

ARGUMENT

If I were freely choosing to do this, it would be because . . .

1. *It's a challenge to take so much information and present it in a comprehensible way.*

2. *I like having an opportunity to relate to my boss more as an equal.*

3. *It's interesting to get to know people in other divisions of the company.*

4. *I'm proud that I can stay impartial in the face of so many clashing views and interests.*

5. *It's fun to play detective and uncover the real situation behind the official version.*

Now it's your turn. . . .

ACTIVITY
   I . . .

ATTRIBUTION
   I did this because . . .

ARGUMENT
   If I were freely choosing to do this, it would be
   because . . .

   1.
   2.
   3.
   4.
   5.

ACTIVITY
   I . . .

ATTRIBUTION
   I did this because . . .

ARGUMENT
   If I were freely choosing to do this, it would be
   because . . .

   1.
   2.
   3.
   4.
   5.

ACTIVITY
   I . . .

ATTRIBUTION
   I did this because . . .

ARGUMENT
   If I were freely choosing to do this, it would be
   because . . .

   1.
   2.
   3.
   4.
   5.

As you read over your responses, here are some
questions to keep in mind:

• Am I discounting or overlooking the intrinsic
  rewards of doing this because I feel I have to
  do it?

• Is this really something I have to do, or do the
  external consequences make me *feel* I have to
  do it?

• If I didn't have to do it, would I *want* to do
  it?

The answers may surprise you. A neighbor of mine
used to grumble constantly about having to walk his
dog twice a day. Then his wife went to visit relatives
and took the dog with her. My friend suddenly real-

ized that he missed the chance to get outside, the leisurely strolls, the casual chats with other dog owners. All he had left to grumble about was that he'd been robbed of a perfect excuse to grumble!

This doesn't mean that we should merely rationalize what we are already doing. Real self-determination involves making choices that lead in the direction of personal growth. It means seeking out reasonably difficult challenges, looking for opportunities to use and develop our abilities and skills, being creative and flexible in our approach to new situations. But the first step from here to there is to begin replacing an overdeveloped focus on external rewards with a heightened sensitivity to the power of intrinsic rewards.

8

THE CAPABLE SELF

Throughout this book, we've been looking at people who seem to have a knack for getting things done. We've tried to understand what it is about them that's distinctive. What we've found is that they:

- expect that they will be effective and succeed [Chapter Three]

- pay more attention to the positive feelings they get from success than to the negative feelings that accompany failure [Chapter Four]

- prefer to take on challenges that are neither too easy to be rewarding nor too difficult to be overcome [Chapter Four]

- see their successes as the result of both temporary and lasting internal causes (effort, ability), and their failures as more the result of temporary causes (effort, temporary external factors) [Chapter Five]

- use partial goals and rewards along the way to keep up their motivation to achieve long-term goals [Chapter Six]

- keep their attention focused on their own reasons for choosing to do what they do and avoid discounting these reasons because of external consequences [Chapter Seven]

(If there are any of these characteristics that you're not quite sure about, take a few minutes at this point to go back and glance over the chapter in which it was discussed.)

One easy way to remember these factors is to think of them as ''An *Ex* and Four *Ins*'':

- High **Ex**pectations
- **In**termediate Difficulty
- **In**ternal Attributions
- **In**terim Goals and Rewards
- **In**trinsic Motivation

These qualities (and the different psychological theories that deal with them) are like snapshots taken from different angles. The subject of all the snapshots is something we can call *The Capable Self*. The Capable Self is a set of interlocked beliefs and perceptions that we hold about our strengths, capacities, and place in the world. At its core is the conviction that we possess the abilities, skills, and energy we will need to have an impact on events that affect our lives. What we do matters. We can make a difference in what happens to us.

The other important characteristics of the Capable Self that we've talked about already are directly connected to that core belief:

- I'll approach new challenges expecting to be able to affect the outcome. If I try, I'll have a good chance of succeeding.

- To make the most effective use of my efforts and abilities, I'll try to stay away from tasks that are either much too easy or much too difficult for me.

- When I do succeed, I'll see that largely as the result of my ability and effort. If I don't succeed, I'll reason that I must not have tried hard enough and that with greater effort, next time I *will* succeed.

- I'll be able to adopt long range goals and plan the steps that will lead to achieving them, because I'm convinced that what I do between here and there will have a real impact on the outcome.

- When there are external reasons for doing something, I'm able to resist the tendency to discount or forget my own internal reasons because I see myself as responsible for my own actions.

"Live As If . . ."

Earlier in the book, at the end of Chapter Two, I suggested that we should adopt as a motto these words:

> Live as if you are already
> The person you want to be.

I also promised to explain what I mean by them. By now, I'm sure you have a very good idea of what they mean, but it may still be useful to spell out the details.

Many psychologists have suggested that we all have a basic need for *cognitive consistency*, that is, we much prefer to act in ways that fit with our general idea of ourselves. If we notice (or we're *forced* to notice) inconsistencies in what we think, say, or do, it makes us uncomfortable, and we try to do something to reduce that discomfort.

- Jenny recently made a small contribution to an environmental action group. When she gets a plea from the group to write to her Congressperson about an upcoming bill, she does so, because she now sees herself as a supporter of the group.

- Artie is convinced that he is a technological klutz. He always asks his ten-year-old daughter to program the VCR and never manages to hear or remember her explanations of how to do it himself.

- Gary prides himself on being fair. When he's asked to evaluate a subordinate whom he personally dislikes, he goes out of his way to give the person a favorable rating.

- Alicia thinks of herself as basically unattractive. When a guy starts flirting with her at a party, she doesn't respond or even seem to notice. Later, when a friend comments about the guy's interest, Alicia pooh-poohs it.

There's a flip side to acting a certain way because we think that we're that kind of person. If we consistently act like a certain kind of person, at some point we may come to accept that we *are* that kind of person.

This is not a totally new insight. In fact, it has a long history in our popular culture. Just think back to the movie of *The Wizard of Oz.* In their actions, Dorothy's three companions displayed exactly those qualities that they were sure they lacked. The Tin Man was sensitive and caring, the Scarecrow thought through problems, the Cowardly Lion was brave when it counted. In their case, it took the intervention of the Wizard, and some harmless trickery, to convince them of what was already obvious to us in the audience.

Here's another example:

> Very early in the year, four-year-old Jason decided that none of his nursery school classmates liked him or wanted to play with him. This led him to hold himself apart and stay out of group activities even when urged to join in. As a result, the other kids quickly learned to ignore him. That, of course, only confirmed his opinion of himself.
>
> When the teacher saw the developing problem, she came up with a clever solution. She invented the new position of Cookie Monitor and appointed Jason to it. Each day at snack time, it was his job to go to each of the other kids, ask them what kind of cookie they wanted, and give them what they'd asked for.
>
> Jason soon noticed that, far from pushing him away, his classmates seemed glad to see him come over to them. His mood improved, and he began to join their games without hovering

around the edge or asking permission. Because he now saw himself as an accepted member of the group, he acted like one and was treated like one.

All of the exercises in this book have the same basic purpose:

- To show you how a Capable individual approaches a particular problem
- To give you practice using that approach yourself
- To help you realize that you are *Capable* of using that approach

The more you train yourself to think, feel, and act like a Capable person, and the more clearly you recognize your growing success at doing so, the more you'll get into the habit of seeing yourself as a Capable Self.

The Uses of Optimism

Whenever I think about the benefits and drawbacks of an optimistic attitude, I recall a cynical friend from college. Anytime something went wrong, he could be counted on to come out with a butchered version of a famous quotation from Rudyard Kipling: "If you can keep your head, when all about are losing theirs, maybe you haven't quite grasped the situation!"

The irony is that unfashionable Kipling was right, and my smart-aleck classmate was wrong. Study after study has shown that people who hold onto an opti-

mistic attitude not only do better at getting things
done, but do so with less stress and more enjoyment.

Whenever we set out to do something—especially
something new—there's a strong chance that we'll
run into problems, obstacles, setbacks, and frustra-
tions. Life, as President John Kennedy liked to point
out, is unfair. The realist takes a long, clear look at
those facts, then either abandons the project before
starting or aborts it at the first serious difficulty. He
or she is left with the cold comfort of knowing that,
"I said it couldn't be done, and see? I was right."

It takes an optimist to keep going *past* the obstacles. What realist could look at the failure rate of new
businesses and then decide to start still another? Imagine what a realist would have said in 1900 to a friend
who wanted to start manufacturing horseless car-
riages:

> "It's a clever idea, but it'll never go anywhere.
> I've read the experts, and they all agree. Our
> roads are designed for horses and buggies, not
> for these contraptions. And what would happen
> when one of your devices ran low on fuel? My
> horse can always find a patch of grass to eat, but
> you won't find spare tanks of gasoline all over
> the landscape, you know. You'd have to carry
> your own. If your machine breaks down, as it's
> sure to do, you'll have to have a supply of spare
> parts with you and be your own mechanic. And
> what about winter? When it snows, I can take
> the wheels off my buggy and put on runners.
> Can you do that with your gadget? Besides,
> there's a huge investment in carriages, horses,
> stables, feed companies, saddleries. People

won't give that up for a noisy, smelly, expensive, untested toy.''

And at the time, in the short run, *the realist would
have been right.*

Doing anything new and different always involves
risk. You may have to put in a lot of effort, over a
long period of time, with no guarantees that your in-
vestment will ultimately pay off. And if what you're
trying to do is really new, you can count on having
to deal with plenty of scoffers and hecklers as well.
It will take a strong sense of yourself as Capable and
a firm belief in the worth of what you're trying to do
to carry you through. No realists need apply.

Now for the good news:

Optimism can be learned.

Of course, some people seem to have been born
with the knack of seeing the brighter side of things
and keeping their hopes up in spite of difficulties. The
ancient Greeks called them ''sanguine,'' and considered them one of the basic human types. In the same
way, some people seem born with musical talent or a
mathematical mind or the gift of gab. Nonetheless,
any of us can learn to sing a song, play an instrument,
solve a problem, or give a speech. And all of us can
learn to bring the benefits of optimism into our everyday lives.

Psychologist Martin Seligman, of the University of
Pennsylvania, started his career with groundbreaking
studies of how unavoidable failure can make us feel
helpless, so that even when success becomes possible,
we don't make the effort needed to succeed. While

investigating this *learned helplessness*, however, he noticed that some people seemed able to resist it. He and his co-workers embarked on a research program designed to find out why.

The key to these people's immunity turned out to be what Seligman terms an *optimistic explanatory style*. Faced with a failure, these people see it as having a temporary, specific, and external cause ("The person I asked to dance said no because he/she didn't feel like dancing at that moment"). Their successes they see as stemming from lasting, general, and internal sources ("The person I asked to dance said yes because he/she had noticed that I'm a good dancer").

If these statements have a familiar ring to you, they should. Seligman's optimistic style has many points in common with the Capable attributional style we studied and practiced back in Chapter Five. These similarities mean that the exercise in Active Argument (pages 130-134) will help you develop, not only that attributional style, but an overall attitude of optimism as well. Try it and see.

When Not To Use Optimism

All those voices telling us to be realistic can't be entirely wrong. There are times and situations in which an optimistic approach is *not* a good idea.

- You're all ready to set off on vacation with the family when you notice that the tread on one of your front tires is badly worn. If you buy a replacement, it'll throw your schedule off and eat up a hundred bucks of your vacation money. Surely the tire's good for a couple more weeks, isn't it?

- On a solitary hike, you stumble across a beautiful deserted lake and decide to take a dip. Once in, you're tempted to swim out to an island in the middle of the lake. You're a pretty good swimmer, and it doesn't look all *that* far.

- You just changed jobs, and you have to roll over your retirement funds. An acquaintance tells you about a penny stock that's bound to triple in the next few months. It's a little speculative, sure, but how can you expect to make big gains without taking some risks?

- As you're dressing for an important job interview, you find yourself reaching for something slightly outrageous. You're tired of looking like Mr./Ms. Dress-For-Success, it'll make you stand out from the other candidates, and the interviewer will surely recognize and value your individualism, right?

- After your shower, you glance in the mirror and notice that that mole on your side looks a little bigger and a slightly different color than you remember it. But it might be a trick of the light. Anyway, is something that small worth the trouble and expense of a trip to the doctor?

All these situations have a substantial *downside risk*. If you make the optimistic choice, and you're wrong, the potential consequences include not getting a job you want, losing most of your savings, and dying an untimely death. The only approach that makes sense in situations of this sort is cool, careful, calculated realism.

On the other hand, what if you're thinking about taking on a project that may be hard but that will bring important benefits if you succeed? If the costs of undertaking it are mainly your time, effort, and disposable resources, and the costs of failing are largely emotional, then choosing to use an optimistic approach will put you well ahead of the game. Your sense of yourself as capable will give you the confidence you need to jump the hurdles in your way.

Notice that, in the last paragraph, I spoke of *choosing* to use an optimistic approach. "Incurable optimists," people who are that way naturally, may not realize that they have a choice. In the kind of situations we were looking at a moment ago, situations that demand realism, such people may end up paying a very high price for their automatic optimism.

You, however, do have a choice. You can look over the situation and *decide* that, in a particular set of circumstances, either a realistic or an optimistic approach makes better sense for you. That flexibility, the power to choose the assumptions you make and the approach you take, is still another important aspect of the Capable Self.

Developing *Your* Capable Self

As we've already seen, all the specific exercises in this book will play a role in building your sense of yourself as Capable. More generally, there are three major aids to developing your Capable Self. These are:

- Listening selectively
- Emulating models
- Mastering new challenges

Listening. No matter how much faith you have in your own ability and motivation, it's nice to hear someone else confirm them. And in those moments when your confidence sags a little, a quiet reminder that you've already proven that you're Capable can help you straighten up and brush away your self doubts. Even the Movers and Shakers—or should I say, *especially* the Movers and Shakers—make a point of having their own personal cheering sections.

Skilled motivational speakers are highly respected and highly paid, as much as $50,000 for a single hour-long speech, because what they do often works. If I persuade you that you can definitely achieve a certain goal, you'll put more effort into it. Right away, that boosts your chances of success. And if you don't succeed at once, you'll persist longer than you would have if I hadn't convinced you. The result just might be that you *do* eventually succeed (and give me part of the credit).

The only thing wrong with this is that the possible gains from being pumped up generally don't last nearly as long as the possible losses from being deflated. It's much easier for people to undermine your sense of being Capable than it is for them to build it up. If I tell you that you can run a mile in four minutes, it doesn't matter how inspirational I am or how convinced you are. The first time you go out on the track with a stopwatch, you'll discover reality.

Now suppose that instead I tell you that you're too uncoordinated to succeed at *any* athletic activity. If you believe me, you'll stay away from athletics. If you do manage to bring yourself to participate, at the first setback you'll hear my voice saying, ''I told you so.'' You'll attribute your failure to your supposed lack of ability—an internal, lasting, and general cause—and you'll give up. Even if you *do* have the basic capacity to do well, your doubts will guarantee that you never find it out.

The moral is, *listen to what others tell you, but listen selectively*. Others can give you valuable insights about what you've done and how it seems to the outside world, but only you are in a position to decide what you *can* and *will* do.

Models. When I was about ten, a cousin gave me a set of biographies of great Americans. The list was pretty typical of the time: Washington, Lewis & Clark, Lincoln, Teddy Roosevelt, Bell, Edison, George Washington Carver, and Clara Barton. Sojourner Truth and Eugene Debs were *not* included.

The stories mostly followed the same pattern. The hero/heroine undertook something that others thought was impossible—defeating the British, inventing the telephone, building the Panama Canal—persevered through constant difficulties, and ultimately succeeded. Washington lost a whole string of important battles before he managed to beat the Redcoats at the battles of Trenton and Princeton. Lincoln suffered defeat after defeat, right up until 1860, when he won the Presidency. Edison and his team tried hundreds of different materials before they found one that they could use successfully as a filament in their new invention, the light bulb.

I read all the books, some more than once. I can't swear that they influenced my psychological development, but it's worth noting that I remember those books when so many others have slipped from my mind. Certainly the authors and editors, and the parents who bought the books, took it for granted that they *would* influence children, by giving them appropriate models to pattern themselves after.

Current psychological research shows that the authors, editors, and parents were partly right and partly wrong. Seeing someone triumph against great odds, through persistent effort, does raise our confidence in our own ability to succeed *if* we think that person is similar to us in important ways. If not, then the effect on our motivation will be much less. We're likely to assume that what applies to him or her doesn't necessarily apply to us. To give an obvious example, if you are a girl with poor parents, finding out that rich blue-blood Teddy Roosevelt overcame his sickly constitution by going to work on a ranch out West won't affect your own self-confidence.

The same holds if the person's situation seems too remote from our own. As a kid, I loved a book called *Two Little Savages* by Ernest Thompson Seton. It told the story of two boys growing up in backwoods Canada in about 1900. They developed all sorts of woodland skills and had a fine old time doing it. They were confident, capable, and adventurous—terrific models for the reader. But their environment was so totally different from my own that I could only admire them. The thought of trying to imitate them never occurred to me.

Exemplary models affect our motivation indirectly as well as directly. When military officers study accounts of past battles, or politicians read biographies of great statesmen, they are looking for more than inspiration. What they really hope to find is practical tips on what to do and what not to do.

In some respects, at least, the problems of government, business, and war are not that different today than they were in centuries past. If you're familiar with the mistakes that Hannibal made in his campaigns against Rome two thousand years ago, it just might save you from making a similar mistake the day after tomorrow. And your awareness that you possess that competence, those tools, will affect your motivation as well.

Most of the time, of course, we don't find our models in books. We look for them in the here and now of our daily lives. Are you feeling a little insecure because you've just started a new job? Look around at your co-workers. Find one whose talents, background, and personality are not too different from your own, but who is experienced, confident, and successful.

Your aim now is to make that person into your mentor. Watch; listen; ask for advice. You don't need to worry that your new mentor will feel taken advantage of. What could be more flattering than knowing that someone sincerely admires and looks up to you? As for you, the more you know about the strategies and tactics of your own field of activity—the "tricks of the trade"—the more strongly you'll see yourself as Capable, with all the benefits that brings.

Mastery. The very best way to strengthen your belief that you have what it takes to succeed is to succeed repeatedly. This is so obvious that you're probably wondering why I bother to mention it. The reason is that this simple formula has some hidden complexities and traps for the unwary.

Let's say that the way you succeed is by choosing tasks that are easy for you. Those are successes, all right, but they don't help your sense of mastery.

Sooner or later—probably sooner—your misguided confidence will lead you to take on something too hard for you, or something that calls for a more sustained effort than the simple tasks you're used to. When success doesn't come easily, you'll quickly lose confidence and get discouraged. You'll end up in a worse place psychologically than where you started from.

Taking on tasks that are much too hard is even more damaging. Repeated failures undermine your belief that you are Capable, especially if they hit you when you're just starting to form that belief. Sure, life is tough, but that's no reason to go out of our way to make it tougher. Throwing a kid in the deep end of the pool is a well-known method for giving him or her a lifelong lack of confidence in the water. So why throw yourself into the deep end?

To best build your sense of mastery, choose to try things that are a *little* hard for you, that involve a bit of a stretch. I know, I've said this before, more than once. Bear with me—this time, I'll try to say it a little differently.

If you try something that's too easy for you, you can do it without trying. If you try something that's too hard for you, you can't do it however hard you try. But tasks in the middle *maximize* the importance of trying. If you put in a special effort, you can succeed at them; if you don't try hard enough, you won't. In other words, these tasks show you that you can choose to succeed—or not succeed. They also make it more likely that you'll see effort (or its absence) as the important cause of both your successes and your failures. That's exactly the pattern of attributions that's typical of the Capable Self.

Developing your Capable Self has a lot in common

with developing your muscles. You build strength and endurance fastest when you work near the upper edge of your current ability. That's where motivation counts the most. Notice that—*your* ability. Not the ability of the person at the next Nautilus machine, or your cousin who's in the same year of college as you, or the field rep whose sales territory borders your own. You're competing against yourself, against your own personal best up to this point. Whatever you're doing, try to do it a little faster, or more cleanly, or more precisely, than you did it last time. And if you succeed, next time set your sights a little higher still.

"What's In It For Me?"

In one way or another, most of this book has been an attempt to answer that question. To summarize very briefly, the person who has developed a Capable Self:

- chooses goals that are difficult but doable
- looks on new tasks as challenges instead of threats
- persists and tries harder in the face of setbacks
- holds onto a Capable self-image after failure
- uses failure as an incentive to develop new knowledge and skills
- develops new, creative approaches to problems
- likes to put skills to use and improve them

- sets high personal standards for accomplishments
- enjoys trying to meet or better those standards
- resists the influence of competition and external criticism
- experiences less stress while trying to get things done
- resists depression
- gets more done, and has more fun doing it

That's quite a list of benefits, isn't it? Maybe you're thinking that they're only available to a lucky and creative few. If so, set yourself this challenge. Over the next few weeks, try to put as much energy into developing your own Capable Self as you would put into developing your tennis serve, figuring out how to use a new computer program, or following the plot twists of your favorite TV show. Then ask yourself if the results are promising enough for you to keep it up. I'm betting that the answer will be an enthusiastic "Yes."

There's no better time to start than right now. Remember that list of goals you developed in Chapter Six? Is there one that seems especially important and appealing to you at this moment? Go back and read what you wrote as specific, concrete steps toward accomplishing that goal. Choose one of them.

Now . . .

Get It Done!

Are you feeling OK about yourself?
Or still playing destructive games?

THE 15-MILLION-COPY
NATIONAL BESTSELLER BY
Thomas A. Harris, M.D.

I'M OK—
YOU'RE OK

00772-X/ $6.50 US/ $8.50 Can

**The Transactional Analysis Breakthrough that's
Changing the Consciousness and Behavior of People
Who Never Felt OK about Themselves.**

In *I'M OK—YOU'RE OK* find the freedom to change,
to liberate your adult effectiveness and to achieve a
joyful intimacy with the people in your life!

*And continue with a practical program for lifelong
well—being with*

STAYING OK
70130-8/$4.95 US/$5.95 Can

by Amy Bjork Harris
and Thomas A. Harris, M.D.

**on how to maximize good feelings, minimize bad ones,
and live life to the fullest!**

Buy these books at your local bookstore or use this coupon for ordering:

Mail to: Avon Books, Dept BP, Box 767, Rte 2, Dresden, TN 38225   E
Please send me the book(s) I have checked above.
❑ My check or money order—no cash or CODs please—for $_____is enclosed (please
add $1.50 per order to cover postage and handling—Canadian residents add 7% GST).
❑ Charge my VISA/MC Acct#_____Exp Date_____
Minimum credit card order is two books or $7.50 (please add postage and handling
charge of $1.50 per order—Canadian residents add 7% GST). For faster service, call
1-800-762-0779. Residents of Tennessee, please call 1-800-633-1607. Prices and numbers are
subject to change without notice. Please allow six to eight weeks for delivery.

Name_____
Address_____
City_____State/Zip_____
Telephone No._____   OK 0696